PARIS
MANSIONS & APARTMENTS
1893
Facades, Floor Plans & Architectural Details

PIERRE GÉLIS–DIDOT
with Théodore Lambert

Introduction to the Dover Edition by
Christopher Drew Armstrong
Director of Architectural Studies
Department of History of Art and Architecture
University of Pittsburgh

DOVER PUBLICATIONS, INC.
Mineola, New York

Bibliographical Note

This Dover edition, first published in 2011, is an unabridged republication of 100 plates from *Hôtels et Maisons de Paris/Façades et Détails*, originally published by Librairies-Imprimeries Réunies, Paris, in 1893. The original French introduction has been omitted. A new Introduction to the Dover edition, written by Christopher Drew Armstrong, has been specially prepared for this volume.

For the present edition, the original plates have been slightly reduced to better fit the trim size. Please note that all 100 plates have been reproduced at 76% of their original size, since this will affect the scales at the bottom of some of the pages.

Library of Congress Cataloging-in-Publication Data

Gélis-Didot, P. (Pierre), b. 1853.
   [Hotels et maisons de Paris. English]
   Paris mansions and apartments, 1893 : facades, floor plans, and architectural details / Pierre Gélis-Didot. — Dover ed.
      p. cm.
   Originally published: Hôtels et maisons de Paris. Paris : Librairies-Imprimeries Réunies, 1893. With new introd.
   ISBN-13: 978-0-486-47700-8
   ISBN-10: 0-486-47700-2
   1. Architecture, Domestic—France—Paris. 2. Facades—France—Paris. 3. Architecture—France—Paris—Details. I. Title. II. Title: Facades, floor plans, and architectural details.

NA7348.P2G4 2011
728.0944'361022—dc22

                      2010043416

Manufactured in the United States by Courier Corporation
47700201
www.doverpublications.com

INTRODUCTION

§ 1. Gélis-Didot's Purpose in Publishing *Hôtels et maisons de Paris*.

The one hundred plates of views, plans, and measured drawings contained in *Hôtels et maisons de Paris* (1893) present the reader with a cross-section of some of the most sophisticated recent domestic architecture in the French capital. The authors of the book, Pierre-Henri Gélis-Didot and Théodore Lambert, were both trained as architects, and their book was intended for the use of professionals, not for tourists or the general public. Many similar publications appeared in the nineteenth century, serving to disseminate ornamental motifs and model plans throughout Europe and farther afield. French buildings of the *Belle Époque* such as those reproduced in *Hôtels et maisons de Paris* inspired the architects who designed the opulent mansions lining Fifth Avenue in New York and the vast American country houses of the Gilded Age. The architects whose work is illustrated in these pages shaped a vision of architecture projected around the world through their involvement in universal exhibitions and in work for the most elite cultural establishments and commercial enterprises of fin-de-siècle Paris.

The choice of buildings illustrated in *Hôtels et maisons de Paris* is far from systematic, but gives a general sense of the character of elite residential buildings of the 1880s and early 1890s located on tony thoroughfares and in the more exclusive neighborhoods around the city. In his preface, Gélis-Didot explains that none of the buildings had been published when he began the project, and that each building represented either innovative solutions to contemporary design problems or incorporated newly developed materials and construction techniques. As the title indicates, the book illustrated private, single-family *hôtel particuliers* and multi-story apartment buildings [*maisons de rapport* or *maisons à loyer*]. Two structures of a non-residential nature round out the selection, a commercial building on the rue d'Uzès [plates 84–85] and an administrative building for the Compagnie des Chemins de fer de l'Est adjacent to the Gare de l'Est [plates 65–68]. What is perhaps most consistent in all these buildings is their modest height: the private, custom-designed houses never exceed five stories above a basement, while the tallest apartment building includes no more than seven stories under the roof.

Overall, Gélis-Didot believed that the architecture reproduced in *Hôtels et maisons de Paris* stood for the spirit of progress that animated contemporary European culture, his publication appearing between the two great Universal Expositions of 1889 and 1900 that showcased Paris to the world and demonstrated the technical and artistic sophistication of the French nation. Though the range of structures illustrated was limited almost exclusively to domestic architecture, it was felt that the design of such buildings required the greatest care in order to best accommodate the needs of modern urban life. The sites illustrated in *Hôtels et maisons de Paris* were highly constrained and sometimes irregular in form, necessitating that the architect develop intricate plans to accommodate the client's life-style and to capitalize on exorbitant land values. Simultaneously, the architect had to be mindful of expense and produce designs that were economical yet appropriate to both the neighborhood and the purpose of the building.

Evoking the important chapters on architecture in Victor Hugo's *Notre-Dame de Paris* (1830), Gélis-Didot described buildings as "stone books" in which the wealth and degree of civilization of their builders will be read by posterity. The type of architecture illustrated in *Hôtels et maisons de Paris* has been read in a number of ways during the past century; for his part, Gélis-Didot sought to capture what he described as a "happy transformation" in the decades prior to his publication, signaling a renewed vitality in the arts. Architects participated in this transformation by close attention to principles of construction, a subject Gélis-Didot felt had until recently been neglected in architectural education. When *Hôtels et maisons de Paris* appeared in 1893, iron was everywhere apparent in contemporary cities, permitting the construction of colossal structures for a range of new purposes. Brick (rarely used in Paris before the late nineteenth century) and glazed ceramic tile also afforded new possibilities to architects. Though the illustrations in *Hôtels et maisons de Paris* are black and white, many of the buildings incorporated vivid coloristic effects through contrasting materials and painted motifs which can only be appreciated on-site or in color photographs.

Gélis-Didot's embrace of modern industry and excitement at the possibilities offered by new techniques and materials were nothing new. From the 1840s, the architect and journalist César Daly promoted the salutary effects of technology on the development of architecture in the pages of the *Revue générale de l'architecture et des travaux publics*, one of the most influential professional journals of the nineteenth century. Similarly, the architect and theorist Eugène-Émmanuel Viollet-le-Duc wrote in his *Entretiens sur l'architecture* [*Lectures on Architecture*] (1858–72) about ways of integrating metal into all kinds of modern buildings and described new structural systems incorporating large expanses of glass and lightweight terracotta tile. Gélis-Didot's book demonstrates how by the end of the nineteenth century such ideas had become common currency in architectural discourse.

§ 2. Architects in *Hôtels et maisons de Paris*.

The 47 buildings illustrated in *Hôtels et maisons de Paris* are the work of some 31 contemporary French architects executed in a variety of historical styles. Listening to the polemics of modernist architects of the early twentieth century such as Le Corbusier, it is easy to be persuaded that the architecture of late nineteenth-century France represented little more than an incoherent hodge-podge of ornamental motifs applied to the surfaces of buildings. The types of façades illustrated by Gélis-Didot perfectly embody the concept of architectural "eclecticism," evoking a non-rigorous embrace of history regarded by critics as the principal impediment to the development of an appropriate style for the modern world. This historicizing approach to design is closely associated with the pedagogy of the École des Beaux-Arts, the elite state school of fine arts in Paris where architecture, painting, and sculpture were taught and which produced many of the most significant architects of nineteenth-century France. Gélis-Didot took it for granted that French architects of the late nineteenth century had mastered the repertoire of stylistic solutions offered by a close study of architectural history and placed little emphasis on this dimension of the buildings he chose to illustrate.

Many of the architects whose work appears in *Hôtels et maisons de Paris* were trained at the École des Beaux-Arts and three became members of that most elite of French cultural institutions, the Institut de France [Jean-Louis Pascal (1837–1920), Charles-Louis Girault (1851–1908), and Victor Laloux (1859–1937)]. Thus, while most of the names associated with the buildings illustrated by Gélis-Didot have little or no resonance today and some are totally forgotten, these designers should generally be regarded as among the vanguard of architects operating in France in the last decade of the nineteenth century. As students of the École des Beaux-Arts, four won of the prestigious *grand prix de Rome* competition, namely Julien Guadet (1834–1908; *grand prix* 1864), Pascal (1866), Laloux (1878), and Girault (1880). A fifth architect whose work figures in *Hôtels et maisons de Paris*, Jacques-René Hermant (1855–1930), came in second to Girault in the 1880 *grand prix* competition. At the time of the book's publication, Guadet, Laloux, and Pascal were all heads of ateliers where architecture students enrolled at the École des Beaux-Arts received practical training as part of their formal education. Laloux, for example, was a *chef d'atelier* from 1890 to 1936, training over 600 French and foreign students in the course of his career. A comparable number of students probably passed through Pascal's atelier between 1872 and 1920. In addition to being a *chef d'atelier*, Guadet served as professor of architectural theory at the École des Beaux-Arts from 1894 to 1908 and authored a major textbook—his four-volume *Éléments et théorie de l'architecture* (1901–04).

Though the houses and apartments illustrated in *Hôtels et maisons de Paris* are relatively minor commissions, many of the architects were involved in more significant commercial and public work. Pascal, the dean of French architects at the moment Gélis-Didot's book appeared, succeeded Henri Labrouste as architect of the Bibliothèque Nationale (1875–1912) and designed the wing encompassing the large oval reading room. Guadet, one of Charles Garnier's collaborators on the Opéra, designed the Central Post Office in Paris (1880–92) and oversaw the reconstruction of the Théâtre Français in the Palais Royal after it burned in 1900. Girault designed the Petit Palais (1897–1900) for the Universal Exposition of 1900 and served simultaneously as the coordinating architect for the construction of the Grand Palais. Hermant, who began his career working with his father Achille Hermant (1823–1903) on buildings such as the apartment houses illustrated in this book [plates 81, 90–92], was catapulted to fame when he won a competition to design the Caserne des Gardes Républicains on the Boulevard Henri IV (1890–1905). Hermant subsequently designed the French pavilion for the World's Columbian Exposition in Chicago (1893) and produced a range of commercial buildings in Paris, most notably the opulent headquarters for the Société Générale banking establishment (1909–10). Laloux produced city halls for the towns of Roubaix and Tours, as well as what is perhaps now the most famous railway station in the world, the Gare d'Orsay (1898–1900), transformed into the Musée d'Orsay in the 1980s.

Other architects of major note whose works are represented in *Hôtels et maisons de Paris* are Lucien Magne (1849–1916), a student of the École des Beaux-Arts who worked with Laloux on the Gare d'Orsay and completed the basilica of Sacré-Coeur de Montmartre after the death of Paul Abadie in 1884. Charles Mewès (1858–1914), who studied under Pascal at the École des Beaux-Arts, went on to a brilliant international career in partnership with the English architect Arthur Joseph Davis (1878–1951), also one of Pascal's students. Together, Mewès and Davis designed the Ritz Hotels in London (1905–06), Madrid (1908–10), and Paris (1898), as well as the Royal Automobile Club on Pall Mall (1910) and luxury steam-ship interiors for the Hamburg-Amerika Line. Stephen Sauvestre (1847–1919), who received his formal education at the École spéciale d'architecture in Paris, was involved in the design of the Eiffel Tower (1887–89) and collaborated with Ferdinand Dutert on the design of the Gallerie des Machines for the Universal Exposition of 1889. Finally Paul Sédille (1836–1900) studied at the École des Beaux-Arts and is best known for designing the flagship building for the Magasins du Printemps on the Boulevard Haussmann (1882–85).

Though Le Corbusier characterized students of the École des Beaux-Arts as hothouse flowers incapable of accepting the advent of new technologies, a number of the architects represented in Gélis-Didot's book enthusiastically took up the use of iron, concrete, and other technical innovations in their work. Sédille's Printemps department store is perhaps the most obvious example of a new building type for a new form of merchandizing, incorporating large iron and glass vaults to light the interior spaces. Both Charles Mewès and Jacques Hermant drew inspiration from the heating, ventilation, and structural systems developed by American architects, the latter visiting Chicago in 1893, where he studied skyscraper technology at first hand. Working with Edmond Coignet, Hermant subsequently pioneered in the use of reinforced concrete in Paris around 1900.

§ 3. The Buildings in *Hôtels et maisons de Paris*.

The buildings illustrated by Gélis-Didot in *Hôtels et maisons de Paris* reveal little about new materials or construction techniques: they appear to be sophisticated exercises in style and in the careful planning of private interior spaces. Since the eighteenth century, French architects regarded the art of "distribution" or interior planning as one of their major contributions to modern architecture. Jacques-François Blondel, an influential teacher in eighteenth-century Paris, published a number of works illustrating the principles of distribution that remained authoritative well into the twentieth century. In *The Decoration of Houses* (1897), Edith Wharton cites Blondel's work among numerous other French publications on interior planning and design, leaving no doubt that at the time of writing France was the leading nation when it came to domestic architecture.

The complexity of interior distribution, especially in elite Paris residences, lay in properly accommodating a variety of conflicting functions ranging from the formal and intimate spaces occupied by members of the family to service spaces such as stables, kitchens, and laundries. The plans of elite residential buildings illustrated in *Hôtels et maisons de Paris* reveal the finely tuned techniques for separating the different individuals who occupied these buildings and for accommodating a range of specialized functions. Covered passages for carriages, courtyards separating the main house from service quarters, and such specialized spaces as winter gardens appear in many of the designs and speak to a heightened desire for comfort and privacy. Strategies employed for reinforcing class boundaries and providing for hygiene may be gleaned from close attention to the organization of spaces and circulation patterns in the building plans. Though these seem to be a minor element of the book, Gélis-Didot notes that the plans throughout are illustrated at the same scale for easy comparison and their individual rooms are labeled, making them legible to a trained eye.

One notable sub-category of residential building included in *Hôtels et maisons de Paris* are houses for artists, three of which may be identified. These buildings attest not only to the special interior spaces and distributions required for work, display, and the transaction of business, but also to the elevated social status enjoyed by elite artists whose residences spoke to their professional success. Gélis-Didot's collection opens with a house at 36 boulevard des Invalides designed by Charles Mewès, which happens also to have been the architect's own residence. The relatively modest exterior—embellished with Mannerist detailing such as rustication and exaggerated voussoirs—suggests a sixteenth-century Italian palazzo [plates 1–2]. The architect's studio and office were located on the ground floor of the building, adjacent to the main entrance. Mewès's house might be compared to Otto Wagner's exactly contemporary house and studio on the Renweg in Vienna (1889), an even more opulent statement of the architect's social ambitions and debt to Renaissance masters.

A similar statement of an artist's professional and social status is the house located at 61 rue Ampère designed for François Flameng (1856–1923), a hugely successful history painter, portraitist, and illustrator elected to the Institut de France in 1905 [plates 27–28]. Though the plans for this house only illustrate the first two floors, Flameng's large, brightly lit studio at the top of the building is apparent in the elevation. Gélis-Didot also illustrated a more modest artist's residence at 7 place des États-Unis [plate 33], which included two superimposed ateliers. The studio on the upper level is accessible both from within the house and by an "escalier des models" with a separate entrance, suggesting the careful segregation of the artist's models from the private domestic spaces. The building was occupied until 1907 by the portrait painter Julian Story (1857–1919), son of the American neoclassical sculptor William Wetmore Story, and was subsequently demolished for the construction of an apartment building.

One of the masterpieces illustrated by Gélis-Didot is the still-extant house at 9 rue Fortuny (1889–1890), designed for an unidentified client by the little-known architect Paul-Adrien Gouny. The façade, embellished with ceramic tiles designed by Jules Lœbnitz, is a riot of color and a manifesto for the artful combination of brick, stone, glass, and metal. The plan reveals deft handling of a complex program: a stable and carriage house is located at the back of the site, separated from the main house by a courtyard. The main rooms of the house are located on the second level, accessed from a covered passage and an elaborate staircase. Variations in size and type of fenestration correspond to different interior spaces. Gouny's disciplined but complex composition integrates polychromatic decoration and a range of materials, the fusion of which would be explored in subsequent years by figures such as Victor Horta and Hector Guillmard.

As architect of the Compagnie des Chemins de Fer de l'Est, Gouny designed a large office building housing the company's legal and accounting departments [plates 65–68]. The building spans a block between the rue d'Alsace and the rue du Faubourg Saint-Denis, presenting distinct façades to each street. The exploration of materials and polychromatic effects that characterize the house designed by Gouny on the rue Fortuny reappear in monumentalized form on the rue du Faubourg Saint-Denis façade. Brick arches, metal lintels, stone quoins, and spindle-thin cast-iron colonnettes frame enormous windows maximizing interior illumination. As a headquarters of a major international railway company, the building proclaims the corporation's desire to project a progressive, modern image.

Gustave Raulin's more modest but equally innovative commercial building facing onto the narrow rue d'Uzes similarly exploits the potential for opening vast surfaces of glass onto the street using structural iron columns and lintels [plates 84–85]. Organized around a large, central, glazed courtyard giving access to a pair of staircases, the building interiors were designed for maximum flexibility and to admit a maximum of daylight. Toilets on each level placed on either side of the main staircase face into small light-wells for ventilation. The elevation recalls the cast-iron commercial façades that proliferated in Soho in New York in the 1850s while the plan recalls much larger commercial structures designed along similar lines in Chicago (such as Burnham and Root's Rookery building), though Raulin seems not to have incorporated elevators. Little is known about Raulin: he studied with the maverick architect Hector Horeau, an early exponent of glass and metal architecture, and served as inspector for the more staid Charles-Auguste Questel on the reconstruction of the Gallerie Doré in the headquarters of the Banque de France (formerly Hôtel de Toulouse).

§ 4. Impact of *Hôtels et maisons de Paris*.

Edith Wharton's statement that French architects of the late nineteenth century were the clear leaders in domestic architecture merely echoed the opinions of other contemporary authors. Even before the appearance of Gélis-Didot's book, the British artist and critic Philip Gilbert Hamerton (1834–94) used one of the buildings subsequently illustrated in *Hôtels et maisons de Paris*—Cahn-Bousson's apartment building at 32 rue du Luxembourg [plates 79–80]—to illustrate his book on *The Present State of the Fine Arts in France* (1892). Writing in the wake of the 1889 Universal Exposition, Hamerton noted that: "The interest of France as a country for the study of architecture is that the art is alive there and national .... This could not, I believe, be said with equal truth in any other country." [p. 76]

French principles were also enthusiastically received by American architects who sought a sophisticated design language to distinguish their work from the crass productions of untutored practitioners. A symptom of the mounting desire among late-nineteenth-century American designers to carve out an elite, professional niche within the mostly unregulated building trades was Ernest Flagg (1857–1947), who studied at the École des Beaux-Arts from 1889 to 1891. Returning to New York where he set up his architecture practice, Flagg wrote about the "Influence of the French School on Architecture in the United States" for the *Architectural Record* in 1894. Embracing order and classical rigor, the picturesque and asymmetrical were anathema to Flagg's sensibilities. He regarded the contemporary fad for Queen Anne styling as irrational and characterized the ponderous masses typical of the Richardsonian Romanesque as a wrongheaded attempt to formulate a distinctive national style. Worse still, ever taller buildings were transforming American cities into ugly, dark canyons hazardous to the health and safety of urban populations. Though Flagg is perhaps now best known as the designer of the Singer Building—the tallest building in the world upon its completion in 1908—he was also instrumental in the development of building regulations for New York City that would curb the excesses of the worst speculators.

What Flagg recommended in his 1894 article was a thoughtful embrace of the underlying principles that guided the best French architects in their work rather than a slavish imitation of French buildings. Without referencing Gélis-Didot directly, Flagg illustrated his article with twelve views taken from *Hôtels et maisons de Paris* [plates 65, 29, 77, 1, 5, 27, 97, 81, 36, 15, 31, 19], each offered without comment as a model of propriety and sophistication that could serve as so many lessons to contemporary American architects. Here was a refined, urbane architecture that built on the past yet responded to the needs of the modern city dweller by incorporating the best planning practices and the newest materials. It was in these more modest works of the most skillful French practitioners that Flagg found the "glorious Renaissance of the nineteenth century."

CHRISTOPHER DREW ARMSTRONG
Department of History of Art and Architecture
University of Pittsburgh

PARIS
MANSIONS & APARTMENTS
1893
Facades, Floor Plans & Architectural Details

Golis-Didot et Lambert d.   MEWES, ARCH^{TE}   Héliogravure Dujardin

HOTEL

36, BOULEVARD DES INVALIDES

DEUXIEME ETAGE

PREMIER ETAGE

ENTRESOL ET BALCON

ENTRESOL

PLAN
DU REZ-DE-CHAUSSEE

0.002 p.m

1 Concierge
2 Atelier
3 Cabinet
4 Antichambre
5 Hall
6 Salle à manger

Echelle de   5 mètres

Gelis-Didot et Lambert d.   MEWES, ARCHᵀᴱ   Héliogravure P. Dujardin

HOTEL

36, BOULEVARD DES INVALIDES

Gélis-Didot et Lambert d   ESNAULT-PELTERIE, ARCH^{te}   Héliogravure P. Dujardin

HOTEL

5, RUE DE MONTCHANIN

PLAN
DU REZ-DE-CHAUSSEE

Echelle de 0.001 p.m.

1 Salon
2 Salle à manger
3 Patio
4 Vestibule
5 Billard
6 Sellerie
7 Ecurie
8 Remise
9 Box

COURONNEMENT DES LUCARNES

PORTE-FENETRE _ DEUXIEME ETAGE

DEUXIEME ETAGE

PREMIER ÉTAGE

Echelle de 1ᵐ ... 0   1   2   5 mètres

PORTE D'ENTREE

Gelis-Didot et Lambert d.   ESNAULT-PELTERIE, ARCHᵗᵉ   Heliogᵗˢ P. Dujardin

HOTEL
5, RUE MONTCHANIN

Gelis-Didot et Lambert d.　　　　　　C. MEWES, ARCH.ᵗᵉ　　　　　　Héliogᵗᵉ P. Dujardin.

HOTEL PRIVE

ANGLE DU COURS-LA-REINE ET DE LA RUE BAYARD

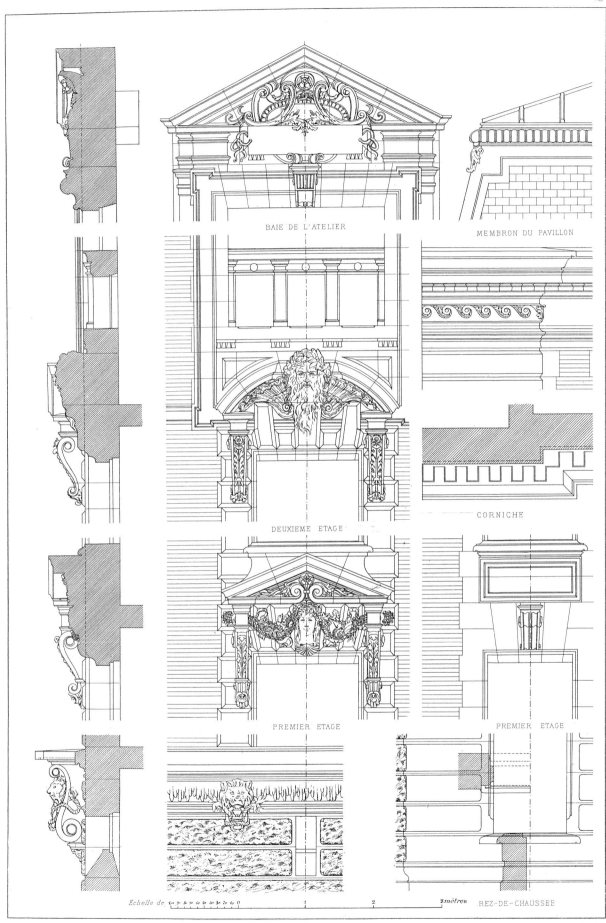

BAIE DE L'ATELIER

MEMBRON DU PAVILLON

DEUXIEME ETAGE

CORNICHE

PREMIER ETAGE

PREMIER ETAGE

Echelle de 0 1 2 3 mètres

REZ-DE-CHAUSSEE

Gelis-Didot et Lambert d.

C. MEWES, ARCH.ᵗᵉ

Héliog.ʳˢ P. Dujardin

HOTEL PRIVE

ANGLE DU COURS-LA-REINE ET DE LA RUE BAYARD

CARTOUCHE DU
VESTIBULE

BAIE DE L'ATELIER

FENETRES
DU
DEUXIEME
ETAGE
D, E

D

CONSOLE

DETAIL DU   FRONTON

E

A

FENETRES DU PREMIER ETAGE

DETAIL DU TYMPAN

B

REZ-DE-CHAUSSEE

A _ Console du Balcon

C

B et C _ Détails
de la Frise

Gelis-Didot et Lambert d   E. MEWES, ARCH.^{te} _ G. GERMAIN, SCULP.^r   Héliog.^{re} P. Dujardin.

HOTEL PRIVE

ANGLE DU COURS LA REINE ET DE LA RUE BAYARD

Gelis-Didot et Lambert d.   L. COCHET, ARCH^TE   Heliogravure P. Dujardin

HOTEL PRIVE

BOULEVARD MALESHERBES ET RUE CARDINET

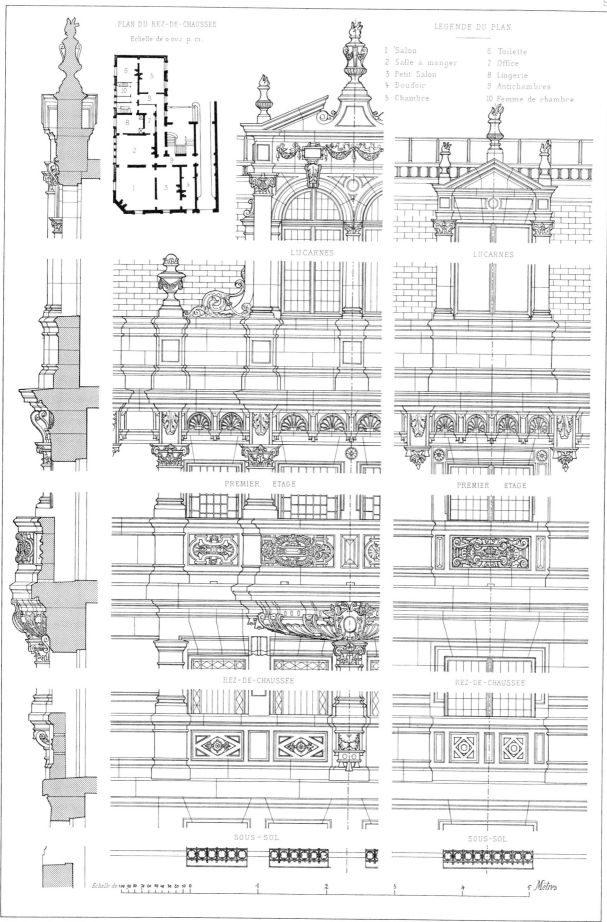

PLAN DU REZ-DE-CHAUSSEE

Echelle de 0.002 p. m.

LEGENDE DU PLAN

1 Salon   6 Toilette
2 Salle à manger   7 Office
3 Petit Salon   8 Lingerie
4 Boudoir   9 Antichambres
5 Chambre   10 Femme de chambre

LUCARNES   LUCARNES

PREMIER ETAGE   PREMIER ETAGE

REZ-DE-CHAUSSEE   REZ-DE-CHAUSSEE

SOUS-SOL   SOUS-SOL

Echelle de 100 90 80 70 60 50 40 30 20 10 0   1   2   3   4   5 Mètres

Gelis-Didot et Lambert, d.   L. COCHET, ARCH.te   Heliog.re P. Dujardin

HOTEL PRIVE

BOULEVARD MALESHERBES ET RUE CARDINET

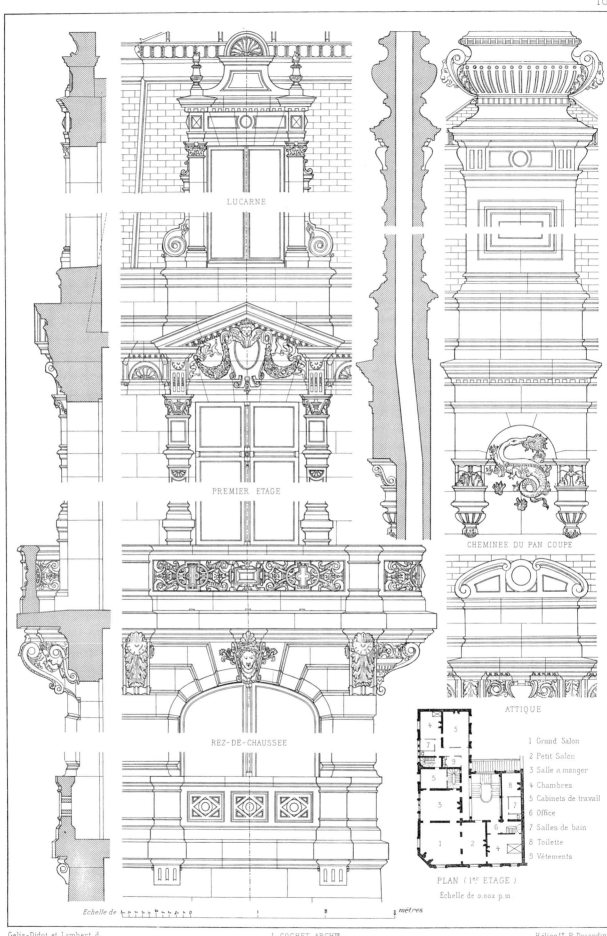

LUCARNE

PREMIER ETAGE

REZ-DE-CHAUSSEE

CHEMINEE DU PAN COUPE

ATTIQUE

1 Grand Salon
2 Petit Salon
3 Salle a manger
4 Chambres
5 Cabinets de travail
6 Office
7 Salles de bain
8 Toilette
9 Vêtements

PLAN (1er ETAGE)
Echelle de 0.002 p.m.

Echelle de   métres

Gelis-Didot et Lambert d.   L. COCHET, ARCHte.   Héliogte. P. Dujardin.

HOTEL PRIVE
BOULEVARD MALESHERBES·ET RUE CARDINET

G. AUBRY, ARCH.ᵀᴱ

HOTEL

22, AVENUE DU TROCADERO

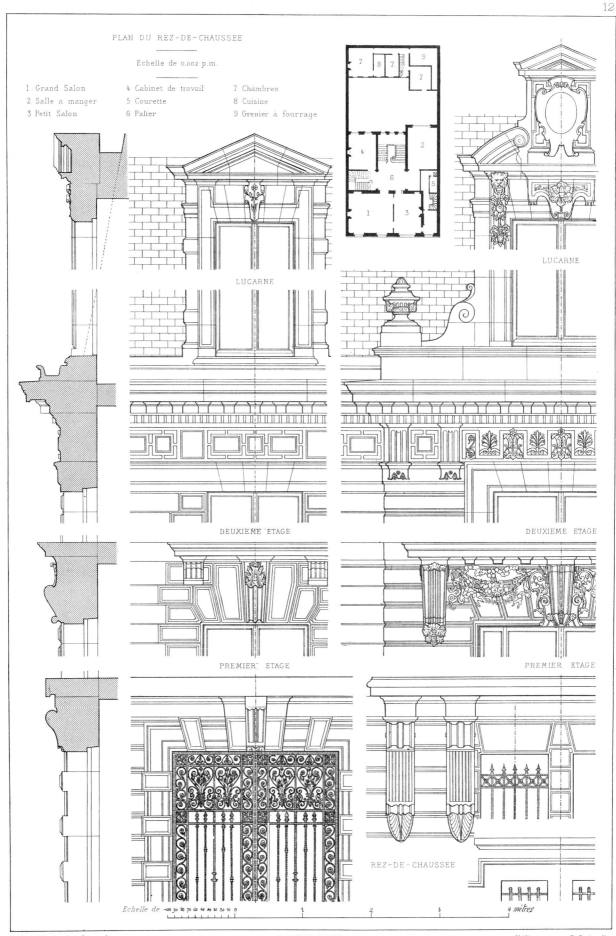

PLAN DU REZ-DE-CHAUSSEE

Echelle de 0.002 p.m.

1 Grand Salon 4 Cabinet de travail 7 Chambres
2 Salle a manger 5 Courette 8 Cuisine
3 Petit Salon 6 Palier 9 Grenier à fourrage

LUCARNE

LUCARNE

DEUXIEME ETAGE

DEUXIEME ETAGE

PREMIER ETAGE

PREMIER ETAGE

REZ-DE-CHAUSSEE

Echelle de ⁻100 90 80 70 60 50 40 30 20 10 0   1   2   3   4 mètres

Gelis-Didot et Lambert d.,   G. AUBRY, ARCH.TE   Héliogravure P. Dujardin

HOTEL

22, AVENUE DU TROCADERO

Gelis-Didot et Lambert d.
ESCALIER, ARCH.^{TE}
Héliogravure P. Dujardin

HOTEL

33, RUE GALILEE

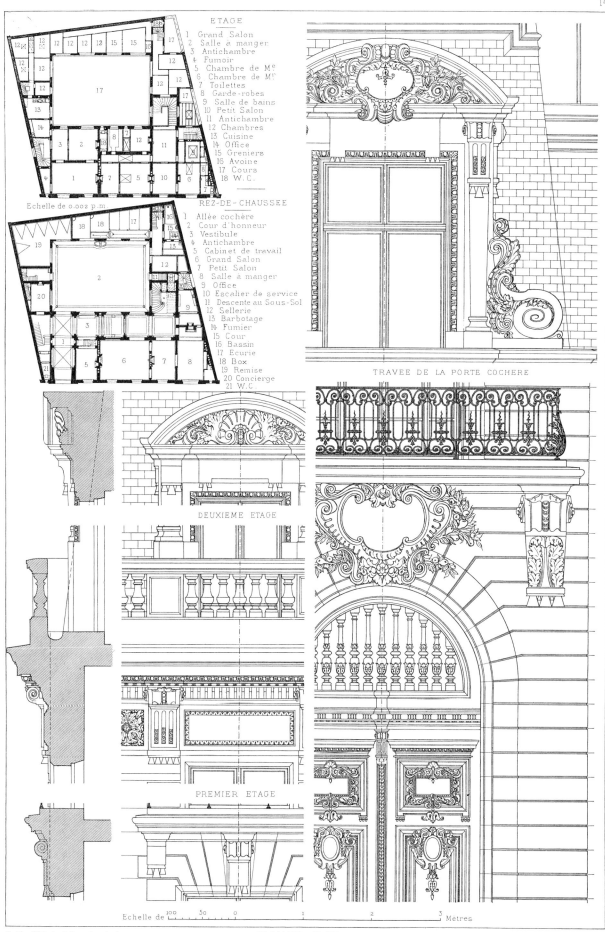

ETAGE

1 Grand Salon
2 Salle à manger
3 Antichambre
4 Fumoir
5 Chambre de Mᵉ
6 Chambre de Mʳ
7 Toilettes
8 Garde-robes
9 Salle de bains
10 Petit Salon
11 Antichambre
12 Chambres
13 Cuisine
14 Office
15 Greniers
16 Avoine
17 Cours
18 W.C.

Echelle de 0.002 p.m.

REZ-DE-CHAUSSEE

1 Allée cochère
2 Cour d'honneur
3 Vestibule
4 Antichambre
5 Cabinet de travail
6 Grand Salon
7 Petit Salon
8 Salle à manger
9 Office
10 Escalier de service
11 Descente au Sous-Sol
12 Sellerie
13 Barbotage
14 Fumier
15 Cour
16 Bassin
17 Ecurie
18 Box
19 Remise
20 Concierge
21 W.C.

TRAVEE DE LA PORTE COCHERE

DEUXIEME ETAGE

PREMIER ETAGE

Echelle de   Mètres

Gelis-Didot et Lambert d.   ESCALIER, ARCHᵀᴱ   Héliogravure Dujardin.

HOTEL

33, RUE GALILEE

Gelis-Didot et Lambert d. L. MAGNE, ARCHᵀᴱ. Héliogravure Dujardin

HOTEL

107, AVENUE HENRI MARTIN

FAÇADE PRINCIPALE

L. MAGNE, ARCHᵗᵉ

HOTEL

107, AVENUE HENRI MARTIN.

FAÇADE POSTERIEURE

PLAN.
DU 1ᴱᴿ ETAGE

0.002 p.m

1. Vestibule
2. Chambres
3. Antichambre
4. Toilettes
5. Cabinet
6. Lingerie

LUCARNE

PIGNON

PREMIER ETAGE

PREMIER ETAGE

REZ-DE-CHAUSSEE

REZ-DE-CHAUSSEE

SOUS-SOL

SOUS-SOL

Echelle de

Gelis-Didot et Lambert d.

L. MAGNE, ARCHᵀᴱ

Héliogravure P. Dujardin.

HOTEL

107, AVENUE HENRI MARTIN

DETAIL DE LA PORTE

CLEF DE VOUTE

BATTUE

SERRURE

VERROU

ENTREE

POIGNEE

DETAILS
au ¼ d'exécution

PANNEAU

PORCHE

PLAN DU REZ-DE-CHAUSSEE

0.002 p.m.

1 Salle à manger
2 Grand Salon
3 Petit Salon
4 Vestibule
5 Porche
6 Entrée
7 Dégagement
8 Office

PORTE D'ENTREE

Echelle

3 Mètres

Gelis-Didot et Lambert d.

L. MAGNE, ARCH.

Héliogravure P. Dujardin

HOTEL
107, AVENUE HENRI MARTIN

Gélis-Didot et Lambert d. PAUL SÉDILLE, ARCH^{te} Héliogravure Dujardin

HOTEL

105, AVENUE DE NEUILLY

FAÇADE SUR LE JARDIN

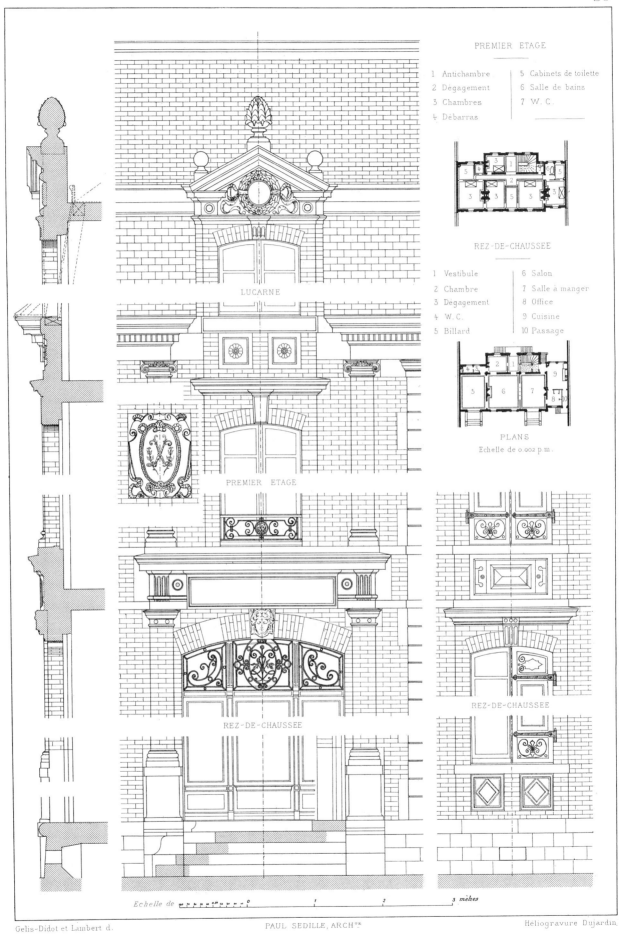

PREMIER ETAGE

1 Antichambre	5 Cabinets de toilette
2 Dégagement	6 Salle de bains
3 Chambres	7 W. C.
4 Débarras	

REZ-DE-CHAUSSEE

1 Vestibule	6 Salon
2 Chambre	7 Salle à manger
3 Dégagement	8 Office
4 W. C.	9 Cuisine
5 Billard	10 Passage

PLANS
Echelle de 0.002 p. m.

LUCARNE

PREMIER ETAGE

REZ-DE-CHAUSSEE

REZ-DE-CHAUSSEE

Echelle de   0   1   2   3 mètres

Gelis-Didot et Lambert d.   PAUL SEDILLE, ARCH.ᵗᵉ   Héliogravure Dujardin.

HOTEL
105, AVENUE DE NEUILLY

Gelis-Didot et Lambert d. L. PARENT, ARCH.Te Héliogravure Dujardin

HOTEL

11, AVENUE DE VILLARS

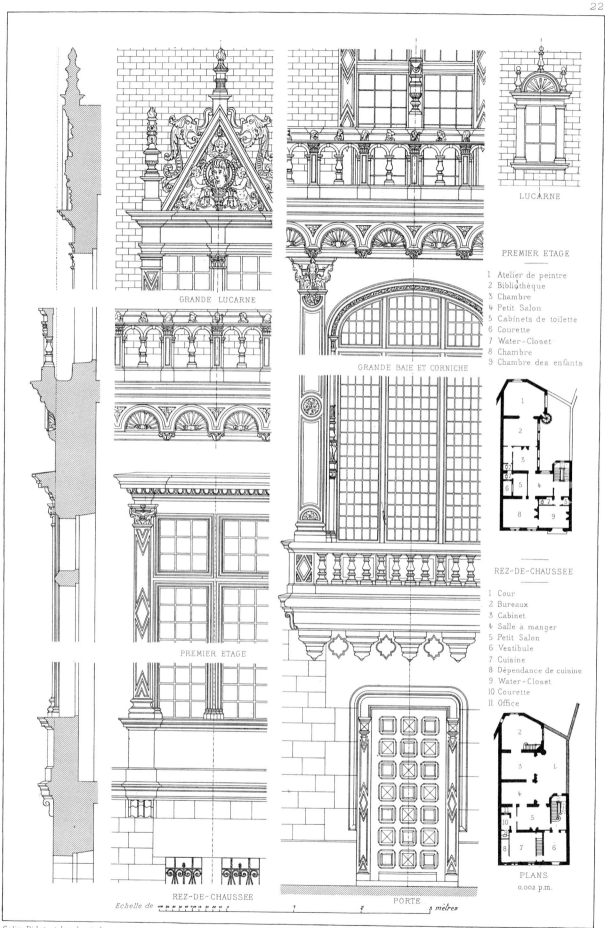

GRANDE LUCARNE

LUCARNE

PREMIER ETAGE

GRANDE BAIE ET CORNICHE

PREMIER ETAGE

1 Atelier de peintre
2 Bibliothèque
3 Chambre
4 Petit Salon
5 Cabinets de toilette
6 Courette
7 Water-Closet
8 Chambre
9 Chambre des enfants

REZ-DE-CHAUSSEE

1 Cour
2 Bureaux
3 Cabinet
4 Salle à manger
5 Petit Salon
6 Vestibule
7 Cuisine
8 Dépendance de cuisine
9 Water-Closet
10 Courette
11 Office

PLANS
0.002 p.m.

REZ-DE-CHAUSSEE

Echelle de   1   2   3 mètres

PORTE

Gelis-Didot et Lambert d.

L. PARENT, ARCH.TE

Héliogravure Dujardin

HOTEL

11, AVENUE DE VILLARS

NICHE _ REZ-DE-CHAUSSEE

TOURELLE

FENETRE DE L'ATELIER

ECHELLE DES DETAILS
0   5o   1 m.

Gelis-Didot et Lambert d.   L. PARENT, ARCH.ᵗᵉ   Héliogravure Dujardin

HOTEL

11, AVENUE DE VILLARS

FAÇADE SUR LA COUR

ECHELLE DES DETAILS
100   0   1 M.

Gelis-Didot et Lambert d.   E. SAUVESTRE, ARCH.ᵗᵉ   Héliogravure Dujardin

HOTEL
116, BOULEVARD MALESHERBES

ESCALIER, ARCH^{te}

HOTEL

RUE DE LISBONNE, RUE DE COURCELLES ET RUE MURILLO

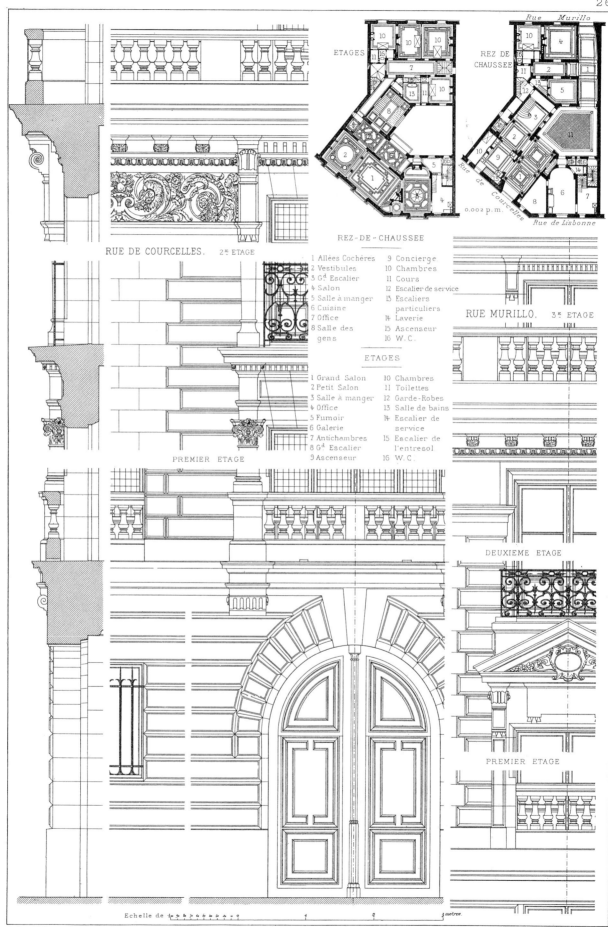

ETAGES

REZ DE CHAUSSEE

Rue Murillo

Rue de Courcelles

0.002 p. m.

Rue de Lisbonne

RUE DE COURCELLES. 2ᵉ ETAGE

PREMIER ETAGE

RUE MURILLO. 3ᵉ ETAGE

DEUXIEME ETAGE

PREMIER ETAGE

REZ-DE-CHAUSSEE

1 Allées Cochéres	9 Concierge
2 Vestibules	10 Chambres
3 Gᵈ Escalier	11 Cours
4 Salon	12 Escalier de service
5 Salle à manger	13 Escaliers
6 Cuisine	particuliers
7 Office	14 Laverie
8 Salle des	15 Ascenseur
gens	16 W. C.

ETAGES

1 Grand Salon	10 Chambres
2 Petit Salon	11 Toilettes
3 Salle à manger	12 Garde-Robes
4 Office	13 Salle de bains
5 Fumoir	14 Escalier de
6 Galerie	service
7 Antichambres	15 Escalier de
8 Gᵈ Escalier	l'entresol
9 Ascenseur	16 W. C.

Echelle de   1   2   3 metres.

Gelis-Didot et Lambert d.   ESCALIER, ARCHᵗᵉ   Héliogravure Dujardin

HOTEL
RUE DE LISBONNE, RUE DE COURCELLES ET RUE MURILLO.

Gelis-Didot et Lambert d.   E. SAUVESTRE, ARCH.ᵗᵉ   Héliogravure Dujardin

HOTEL D'ARTISTE

61, RUE AMPERE

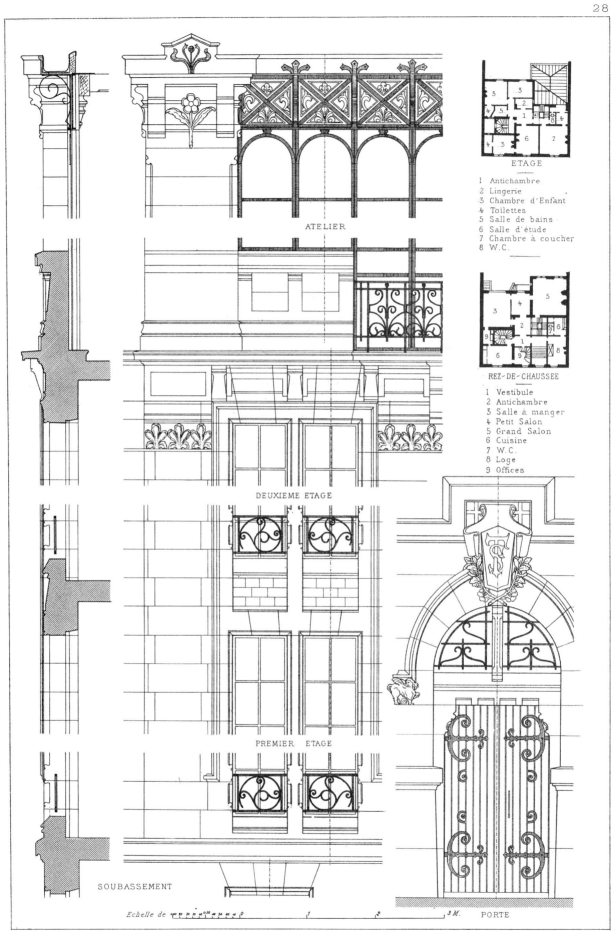

ATELIER

ETAGE

1 Antichambre
2 Lingerie
3 Chambre d'Enfant
4 Toilettes
5 Salle de bains
6 Salle d'étude
7 Chambre à coucher
8 W.C.

REZ-DE-CHAUSSEE

1 Vestibule
2 Antichambre
3 Salle à manger
4 Petit Salon
5 Grand Salon
6 Cuisine
7 W.C.
8 Loge
9 Offices

DEUXIEME ETAGE

PREMIER ETAGE

SOUBASSEMENT

PORTE

Echelle de   0   1   2   3 M.

Gelis-Didot et Lambert d.   SAUVESTRE, ARCH.^{te}   Héliogravre Dujardin

HOTEL D'ARTISTE

61, RUE AMPERE

GOUNY, ARCH^TE

HOTEL

9, RUE FORTUNY

1 Remise
2 Ecurie
3 Fumier
4 Porche
5 Sellerie
6 Cour
7 Cuisine
8 Office
9 Concierge
10 Cabinet de M.

REZ DE CHAUSSEE

1 Petit Salon
2 Grand Salon
3 Dégagements
4 Salle à manger
5 Office
6 W.C.

1ᵉʳ ETAGE

ECHELLE DES PLANS: 0.002 p.m.

1 Terrasse
2 W.C.
3 Cabinet de travail
4 Chambre du fils
5 Toilettes
6 Dégagement
7 Chambre de Mᵐᵉ
8 Chambre de M.

2ᵉ ETAGE

LUCARNE

PETITE SERRE VITRÉE

PORTE D'ENTRÉE

DEUXIEME ETAGE ET COURONNEMENT

PREMIER ETAGE

Echelle de ___ 3 Mètres

Gelis-Didot et Lambert d.   GOUNY, ARCHᵗᵉ   Héliogravure Dujardin

HOTEL

9, RUE FORTUNY

SANSBŒUF, ARCH.ᵀᴱ

HOTEL

52, RUE DE BASSANO

DEUXIEME ETAGE

DEUXIEME ETAGE

1881

PREMIER ETAGE

PREMIER ETAGE

PORTE D'ENTREE

REZ-DE-CHAUSSEE

PREMIER ETAGE
0,002 p.m.

1 Salon de M.
2 Grand Salon
3 Salon de Mᵐᵉ
4 Grande galerie.
5 Escalier du Iᵉʳ.
6 Grand Escalier
7 Salle à manger
8 Office
9 Petite serre
10 Grande serre.
11 Domestiques.
12 Débarras
13 Escalier de service.

Echelle de 100 90 80 70 60 50 40 30 20 10 0 ... 1 ... 2 ... 3 Mètres

Gelis-Didot et Lambert d.

SANSBŒUF, ARCHᵀᵉ

Héliogravure Dujardin

HOTEL

52, RUE DE BASSANO

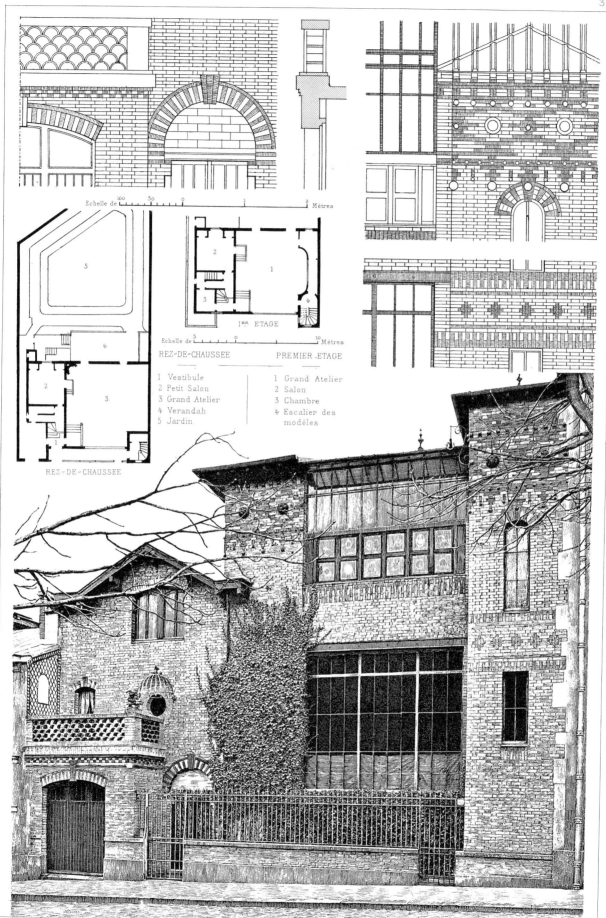

Echelle de 100 50 0 1 2 Mètres

1ᴱᴿ ETAGE

Echelle de 5 0 10 Mètres

REZ-DE-CHAUSSEE   PREMIER ETAGE

1   Vestibule   1   Grand Atelier
2   Petit Salon   2   Salon
3   Grand Atelier   3   Chambre
4   Verandah   4   Escalier des
5   Jardin   modèles

REZ-DE-CHAUSSEE

Gelis-Didot et Lambert d.   CH. GIRAULT ARCHᵀᴱ   Héliogᵗᵉ Dujardin

HOTEL D'ARTISTE

7, PLACE DES ETATS-UNIS.

Gélis-Didot et Lambert d.　　　　　MERCIER, ARCH.ᵀᴱ　　　　　Héliogravure Dujardin

HOTEL

28, RUE DE NAPLES

A

A_REZ-DE-CHAUSSEE

1 Vestibule
2 Vestiaire
3 Grand Salon
4 Petit Salon
5 Salle à manger
6 Jardin d'hiver
7 Office
8 W.C.
9 Courettes

B

B_ETAGE

1 Grande chambre à coucher
2 Chambre à coucher
3 Cabinet de toilette
4 Antichambre
5 Lingerie
6 Salle de bains
7 W.C.
8 Serre
9 Courettes

C

ECHELLE DES PLANS
0.002 p.m.

C _ COMBLES

1 Dégagement
2 Chambre d'ami

3 Chambres à coucher
4 Linge sale
5 Atelier
6 Loggia
7 Débarras
8 W.C.
9 Cour

COMBLES

ETAGE

REZ-DE-CHAUSSEE

TRAVEE DE LA PORTE D'ENTREE

Echelle de 0 1 2 3 Mètres

Gelis-Didot et Lambert d.

MERCIER, ARCH.TE

Héliogravure Dujardin

HOTEL

28, RUE DE NAPLES

PLAN DU 1ᴱᴿ ETAGE

1. Chambre de M.
2. Toilette
3. Chambre de Mᵐᵉ
4. Toilette
5. Chambre de M.Mᵉˡˡᵉˢ
6. Toilettes et garde-robes
7. Garde-robes
8. Débarras
9. W.C.
10. Grenier à fourrage
11. Chambres
12. Fosse à fumier couverte

Echelle de 0.002 p.m.

ECHELLE DES DETAILS

Gèlis-Didot et Lambert d.   P. DECHARD, ARCHᵀᴱ   Heliogravure Dujardin

HOTEL

19, AVENUE MARCEAU

Gelis-Didot et Lambert d.　　　　　　　A. WALWEIN, ARCH.ᵀᴱ　　　　　　　Heliogravure Dujardin

HOTEL

77, RUE DE LA FAISANDERIE

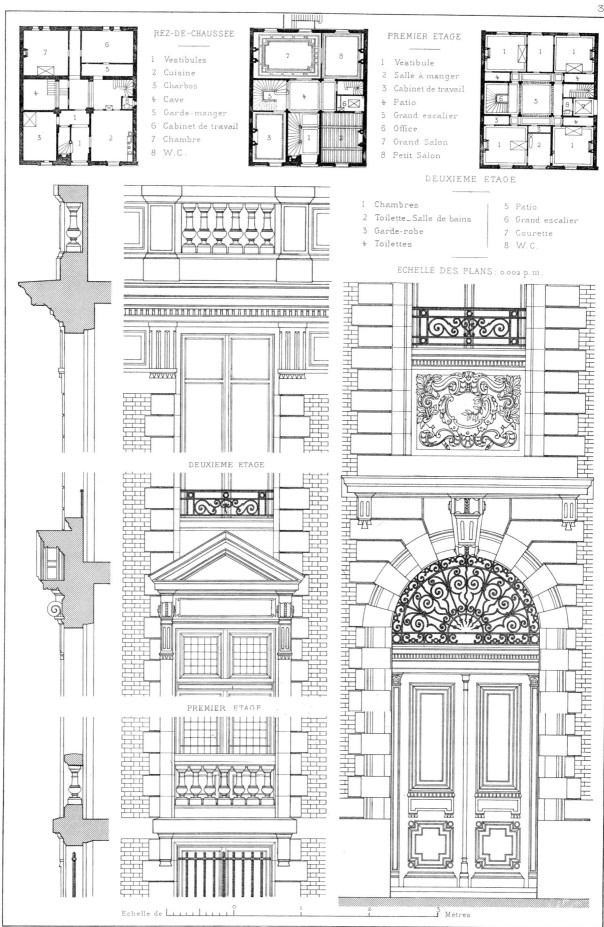

REZ-DE-CHAUSSEE

1 Vestibules
2 Cuisine
3 Charbon
4 Cave
5 Garde-manger
6 Cabinet de travail
7 Chambre
8 W.C.

PREMIER ETAGE

1 Vestibule
2 Salle à manger
3 Cabinet de travail
4 Patio
5 Grand escalier
6 Office
7 Grand Salon
8 Petit Salon

DEUXIEME ETAGE

1 Chambres   5 Patio
2 Toilette_Salle de bains   6 Grand escalier
3 Garde-robe   7 Courette
4 Toilettes   8 W.C.

ECHELLE DES PLANS : 0.002 p.m.

DEUXIEME ETAGE

PREMIER ETAGE

Echelle de 0 1 2 3 Mètres

Gelis-Didot et Lambert d.   A. WALWEIN, ARCH^{te}   Héliogravure P. Dujardin

HOTEL

77, RUE DE LA FAISANDERIE

Gelis-Didot et Lambert d.   A. WALWEIN, ARCH.ᵀᴱ   Héliogravure Dujardin

HOTEL

6, RUE GALILEE

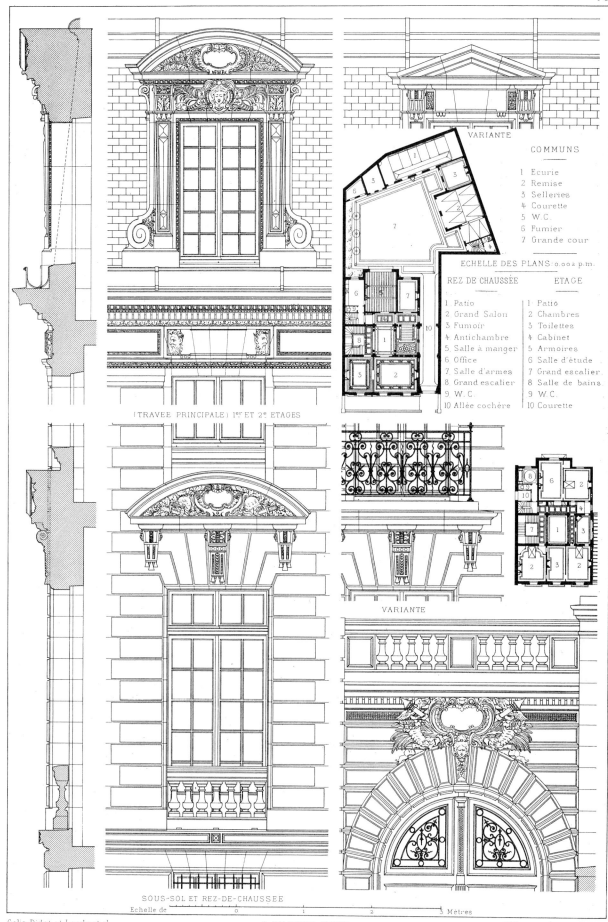

VARIANTE

COMMUNS

1. Ecurie
2. Remise
3. Selleries
4. Courette
5. W.C.
6. Fumier
7. Grande cour

ECHELLE DES PLANS: 0.002 p.m.

REZ DE CHAUSSÉE

1. Patio
2. Grand Salon
3. Fumoir
4. Antichambre
5. Salle à manger
6. Office
7. Salle d'armes
8. Grand escalier
9. W.C.
10. Allée cochère

ETAGE

1. Patio
2. Chambres
3. Toilettes
4. Cabinet
5. Armoires
6. Salle d'étude
7. Grand escalier
8. Salle de bains
9. W.C.
10. Courette

(TRAVEE PRINCIPALE) 1ᵉʳ ET 2ᵉ ETAGES

VARIANTE

SOUS-SOL ET REZ-DE-CHAUSSEE

Echelle de   0   1   2   3 Metres

Gelis-Didot et Lambert d.   A. WALWEIN, ARCHᵗᵉ   Héliogravure P. Dujardin

HOTEL

6, RUE GALILEE

Gelis-Didot et Lambert d.　　　　L. MAGNE, ARCH^{TE}　　　　Héliogravure Dujardin

HOTEL
42 et 44, AVENUE DE VILLIERS

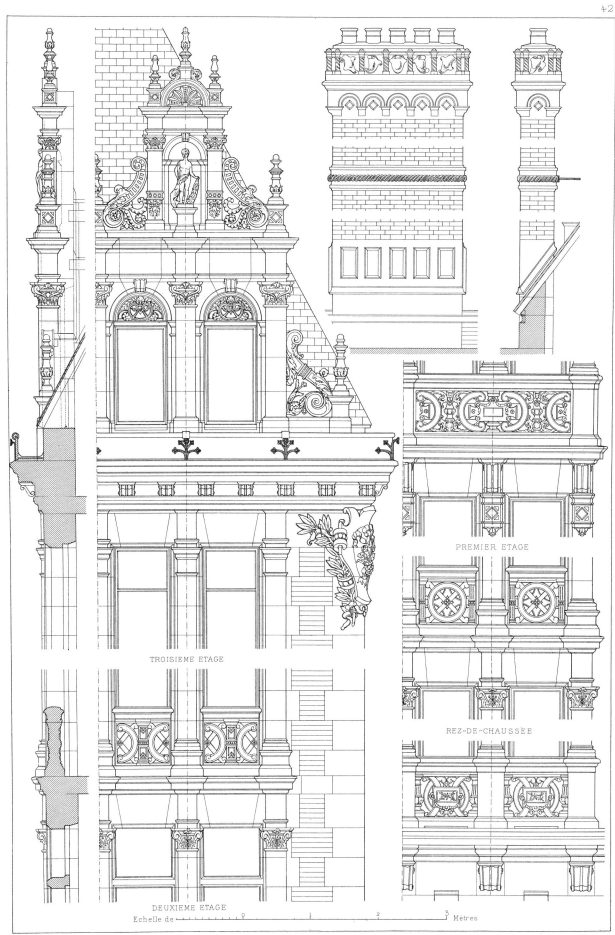

PREMIER ETAGE

REZ-DE-CHAUSSEE

TROISIEME ETAGE

DEUXIEME ETAGE

Echelle de |⊥⊥⊥⊥⊥⊥| 0   1   2   3 Mètres

Gelis-Didot et Lambert d.   L. MAGNE, ARCH^TE   Héliogravure Dujardin

HOTEL

42 ET 44, AVENUE DE VILLIERS

PLAN DU REZ-DE-CHAUSSEE

Echelle de 0.002 p.m.

1 Grand Salon
2 Salon
3 Petit Salon
4 Salle à manger
5 Galeries
6 Bibliothèque
7 Fumoir

8 Offices
9 W.C
10 Courette
11 Cours
12 Ecuries
13 Remises
14 Selleries

FENETRE SUR LE PASSAGE

ENTREE DU PETIT HOTEL

REZ-DE-CHAUSSEE

1880

Echelle de ⊢⊢⊢⊢⊢⊢⊢⊢⊢ 0   1   2   3 mètres

Gelis-Didot et Lambert d.   L. MAGNE, ARCHᵀᴱ   Heliogravure Dujardin

HOTEL
42 ET 44, AVENUE DE VILLIERS

Gelis-Didot et Lambert d.

ESCALIER, ARCH.ᵗᵉ

Heliogravure Dujardin

HOTEL

47, AVENUE DU BOIS-DE-BOULOGNE

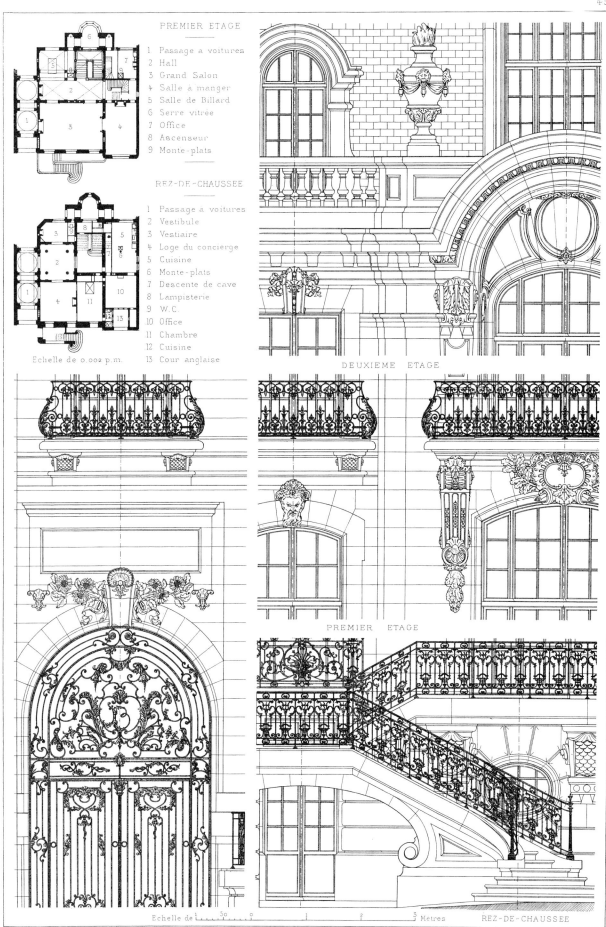

PREMIER ETAGE

1 Passage a voitures
2 Hall
3 Grand Salon
4 Salle a manger
5 Salle de Billard
6 Serre vitrée
7 Office
8 Ascenseur
9 Monte-plats

REZ-DE-CHAUSSEE

1 Passage a voitures
2 Vestibule
3 Vestiaire
4 Loge du concierge
5 Cuisine
6 Monte-plats
7 Descente de cave
8 Lampisterie
9 W.C.
10 Office
11 Chambre
12 Cuisine
13 Cour anglaise

Echelle de 0.002 p.m.

DEUXIEME ETAGE

PREMIER ETAGE

REZ-DE-CHAUSSEE

Echelle de   50   Metres

Gelis-Didot et Lambert d.   ESCALIER, ARCH.™   Heliogravure Dujardin

HOTEL
47, AVENUE DU BOIS-DE-BOULOGNE

1 Grand vestibule
2 Loge du concierge
3 Cuisine, Salle à
   manger des gens
4 Grand Escalier
5 Office
6 Cuisine
7 Débarras
8 Cabinet de
   travail

REZ-DE-CHAUSSEE

1 Antichambre
2 Salon
3 Salle à manger
4 Office
5 Salle de Billard
6 Chambre
7 Divan

PREMIER ETAGE

1 Antichambre
2 Chambre
3 Chambre
4 Cabinet de
   toilette
5 Salle de bain
6 Cabinet de toilette

DEUXIEME ETAGE

Echelle de 0.003 p.m.

Gelis-Didot et Lambert d.   G. DEZERMAUX, ARCH.ᵗᵉ   Héliogravure Dujardin.

HOTEL
28, RUE BALLU

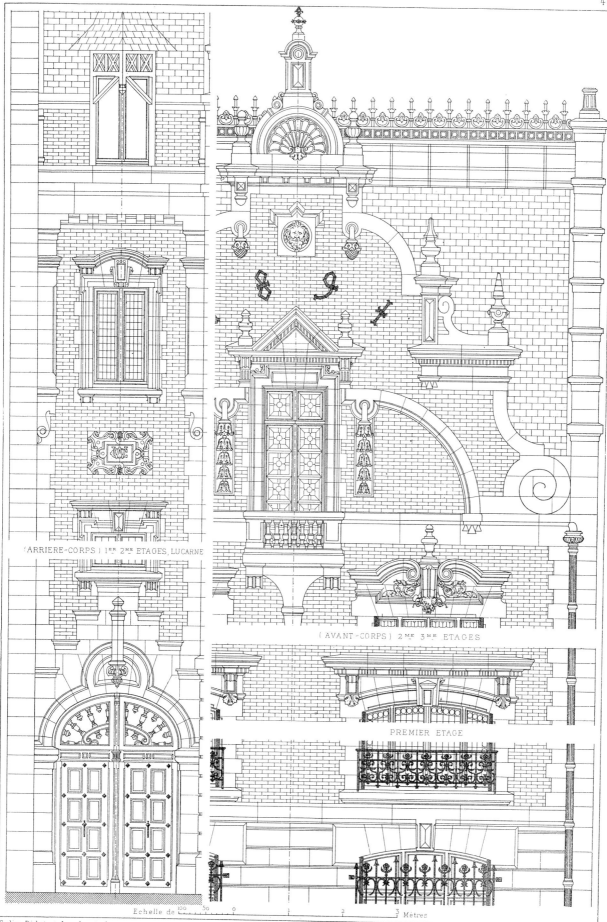

(ARRIERE-CORPS) 1ᵉʳ 2ᴹᴱ ETAGES, LUCARNE

(AVANT-CORPS) 2ᴹᴱ 3ᴹᴱ ETAGES

PREMIER ETAGE

Echelle de 100 50 0 1 2 3 Metres

Gelis-Didot et Lambert d.   G. DEZERMAUX, ARCHᵀᴱ   Héliogravure Dujardin

HOTEL
28, RUE BALLU

Gelis-Didot et Lambert d.

P. GELIS-DIDOT ET TH. LAMBERT, ARCH.^{TES}

Héliogravure Dujardin

MAISON

AVENUE DE SEGUR ET AVENUE DE SAXE

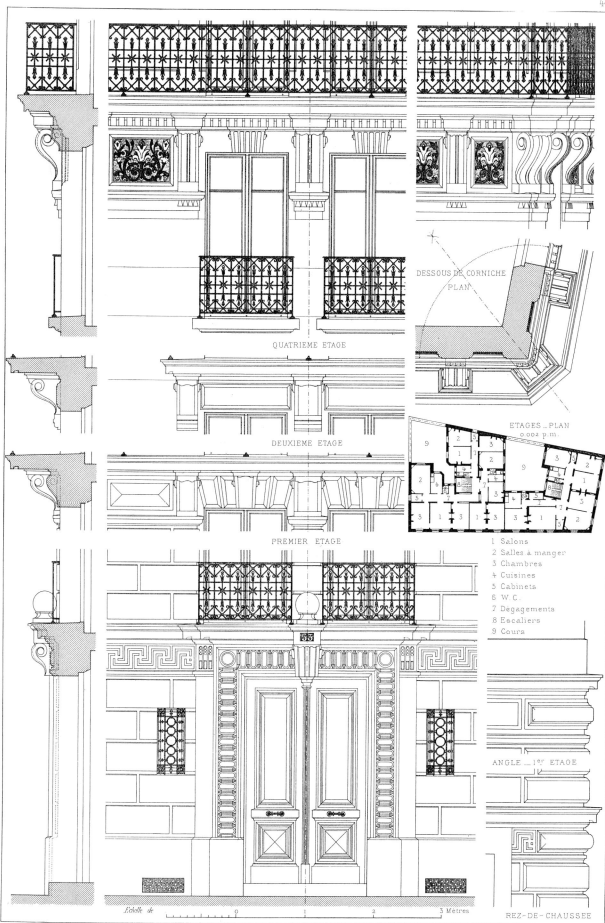

QUATRIEME ETAGE

DESSOUS DE CORNICHE
PLAN

DEUXIEME ETAGE

ETAGES _ PLAN
0.002 p.m.

PREMIER ETAGE

1 Salons
2 Salles à manger
3 Chambres
4 Cuisines
5 Cabinets
6 W.C.
7 Degagements
8 Escaliers
9 Cours

53

ANGLE _ 1er ETAGE

Echelle de   0   1   2   3 Mètres

REZ-DE-CHAUSSEE

Gelis-Didot et Lambert d.   P. GELIS-DIDOT ET TH. LAMBERT, ARCHᵗᵉˢ   Héliogavure Dujardin

MAISON
AVENUE DE SEGUR ET AVENUE DE SAXE

Gelis-Didot et Lambert d. DAINVILLE ARCH.ᵀᴱ Héliogravure Dujardin

MAISON
12, RUE PIERRE CHARRON

AVANT-CORPS

DEUXIEME ETAGE

LUCARNE

PREMIER ETAGE

DEUXIEME ETAGE

ENTRESOL

PREMIER ETAGE

REZ-DE-CHAUSSEE

Echelle de   100   50   0   1   2   3   Mètres

Gelis-Didot et Lambert d.   DAINVILLE, ARCH^{te}   Heliogravure Dujardin

MAISON
12, RUE PIERRE CHARRON

Gelis-Didot et Lambert d. G. VERA, ARCH.ᵗᵉ Heliogravure Dujardin

MAISON

12, RUE DE LA POMPE

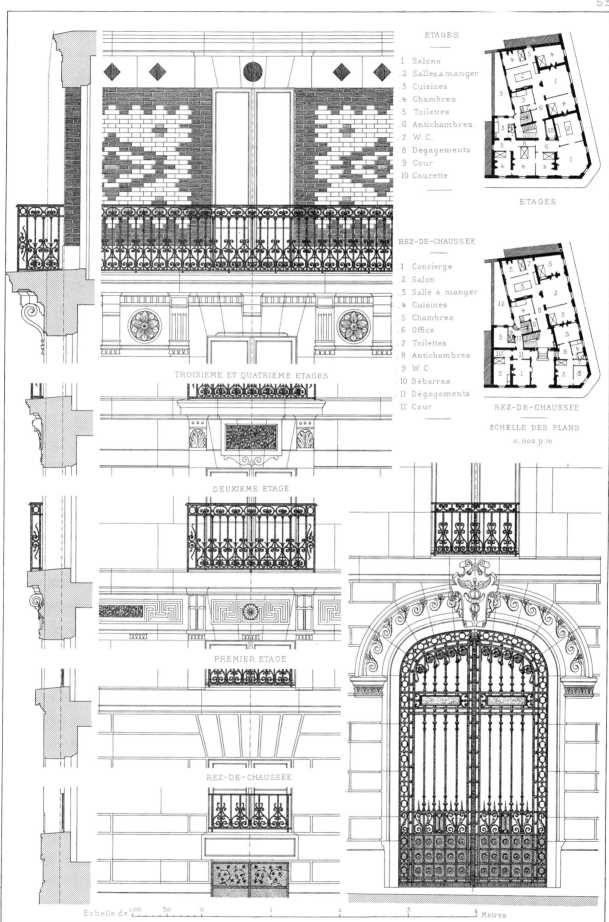

ETAGES

.1 Salons
.2 Salles à manger
.3 Cuisines
.4 Chambres
.5 Toilettes
.6 Antichambres.
.7 W.C.
.8 Dégagements
.9 Cour
.10 Courette

ETAGES

REZ-DE-CHAUSSEE

.1 Concierge
.2 Salon
.3 Salle à manger
.4 Cuisines
.5 Chambres
.6 Office
.7 Toilettes
.8 Antichambres
.9 W.C.
.10 Débarras
.11 Dégagements
.12 Cour

REZ-DE-CHAUSSEE

ECHELLE DES PLANS
0.002 p.m

TROISIEME ET QUATRIEME ETAGES

DEUXIEME ETAGE

PREMIER ETAGE

REZ-DE-CHAUSSEE

Echelle de 1.00   50   0   1   2   3   4 Mètres

Gelis-Didot et Lambert d.   G. VERA, ARCH.te   Héliogravure Dujardin

MAISON

12, RUE DE LA POMPE

Gélis-Didot et Lambert d. BREASSON, ARCH^{TE} Héliogravure Dujardin

MAISON

12 AVENUE DU TROCADERO

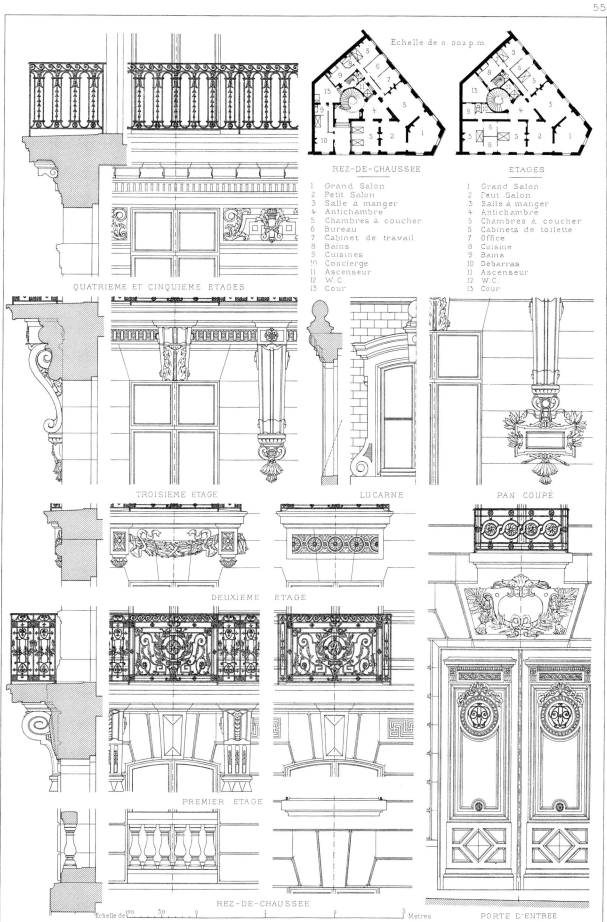

Echelle de 0.002 p.m.

REZ-DE-CHAUSSEE

1 Grand Salon
2 Petit Salon
3 Salle à manger
4 Antichambre
5 Chambres à coucher
6 Bureau
7 Cabinet de travail
8 Bains
9 Cuisines
10 Concierge
11 Ascenseur
12 W.C.
13 Cour

ETAGES

1 Grand Salon
2 Petit Salon
3 Salle à manger
4 Antichambre
5 Chambres à coucher
6 Cabinets de toilette
7 Office
8 Cuisine
9 Bains
10 Débarras
11 Ascenseur
12 W.C.
13 Cour

QUATRIEME ET CINQUIEME ETAGES

TROISIEME ETAGE

LUCARNE

PAN COUPÉ

DEUXIEME ETAGE

PREMIER ETAGE

REZ-DE-CHAUSSEE

Echelle de 100 50 0 1 2 3 Mètres

PORTE D'ENTREE

Gelis-Didot et Lambert d.   BREASSON, ARCHᵗᵉ   Héliogravure Dujardin

MAISON

12, AVENUE DU TROCADERO

Gelis-Didot et Lambert d.   A. WALWEIN, ARCH??   Héliogravure Dujardin

MAISON
43, RUE DE LA POMPE ET RUE DE SIAM

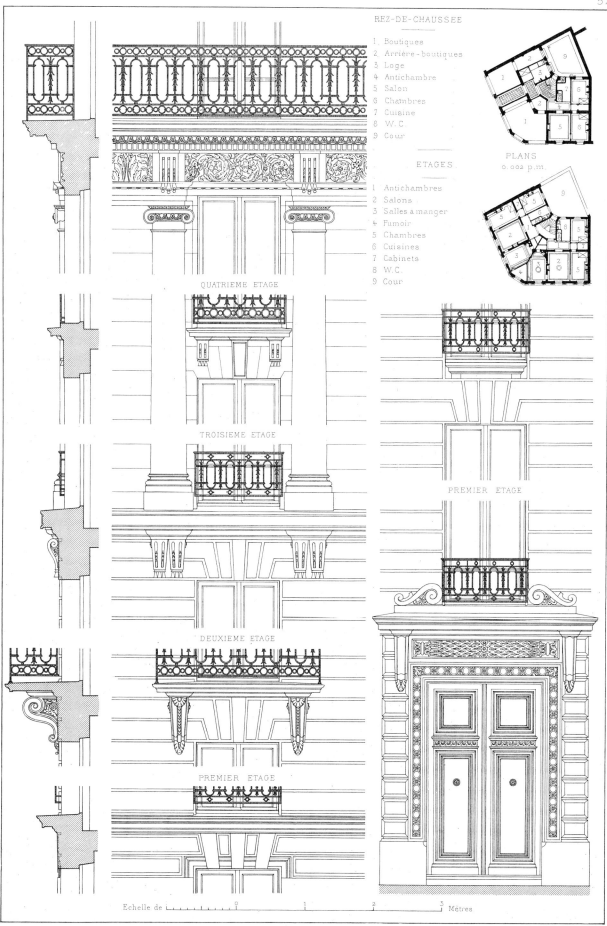

REZ-DE-CHAUSSEE

1. Boutiques
2. Arrière-boutiques
3. Loge
4. Antichambre
5. Salon
6. Chambres
7. Cuisine
8. W.C.
9. Cour

ETAGES.

1. Antichambres
2. Salons
3. Salles a manger
4. Fumoir
5. Chambres
6. Cuisines
7. Cabinets
8. W.C.
9. Cour

PLANS
o.oo2 p.m.

QUATRIEME ETAGE

TROISIEME ETAGE

DEUXIEME ETAGE

PREMIER ETAGE

PREMIER ETAGE

Echelle de 0 1 2 3 Mètres

Gelis-Didot et Lambert d.   A. WALWEIN, ARCH.TE   Héliogravure Dujardin

MAISON

43, RUE DE LA POMPE ET RUE DE SIAM.

A. WALWEIN, ARCH.ᵗᵉ

MAISON

8, RUE DE SIAM

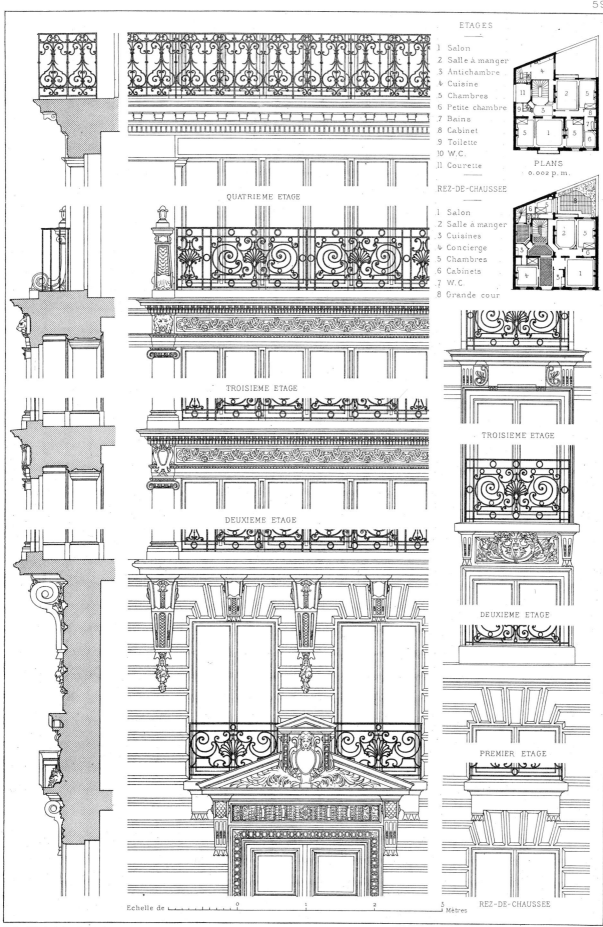

ETAGES

1 Salon
2 Salle à manger
3 Antichambre
4 Cuisine
5 Chambres
6 Petite chambre
7 Bains
8 Cabinet
9 Toilette
10 W.C.
11 Courette

PLANS
0.002 p. m.

REZ-DE-CHAUSSEE

1 Salon
2 Salle à manger
3 Cuisines
4 Concierge
5 Chambres
6 Cabinets
7 W.C.
8 Grande cour

QUATRIEME ETAGE

TROISIEME ETAGE

DEUXIEME ETAGE

TROISIEME ETAGE

DEUXIEME ETAGE

PREMIER ETAGE

REZ-DE-CHAUSSEE

Echelle de 0 1 2 3 Mètres

Gelis-Didot et Lambert d.   A. WALWEIN, ARCH^{te}   Héliogravure Dujardin

MAISON
8, RUE DE SIAM

Gelis-Didot et Lambert d.   CH. GIRAULT, ARCHᵀᴱ   Héliogravure Dujardin

MAISON

12 ᵇⁱˢ PLACE DE LABORDE

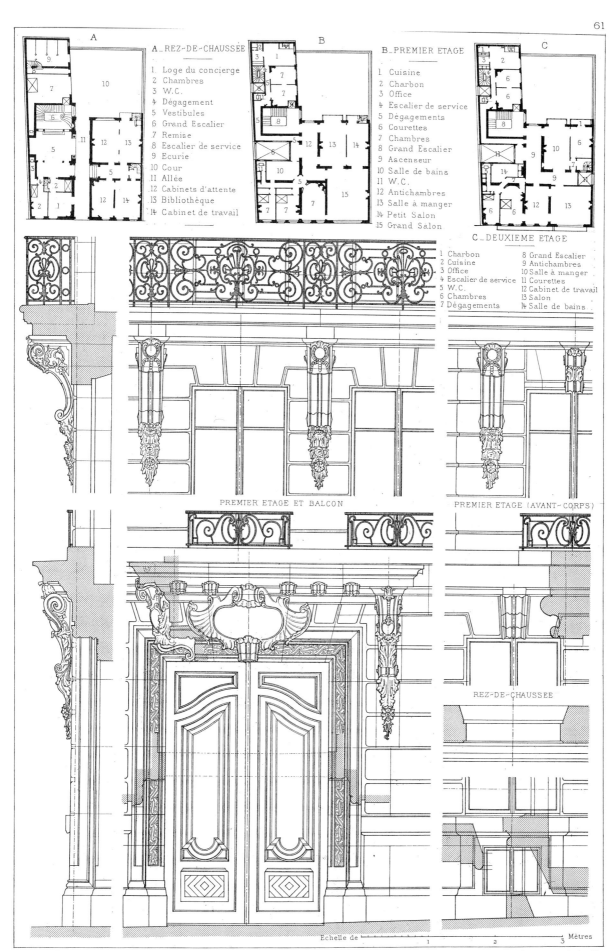

A_REZ-DE-CHAUSSÉE

1. Loge du concierge
2. Chambres
3. W.C.
4. Dégagement
5. Vestibules
6. Grand Escalier
7. Remise
8. Escalier de service
9. Ecurie
10. Cour
11. Allée
12. Cabinets d'attente
13. Bibliothèque
14. Cabinet de travail

B_PREMIER ETAGE

1. Cuisine
2. Charbon
3. Office
4. Escalier de service
5. Dégagements
6. Courettes
7. Chambres
8. Grand Escalier
9. Ascenseur
10. Salle de bains
11. W.C.
12. Antichambres
13. Salle à manger
14. Petit Salon
15. Grand Salon

C_DEUXIEME ETAGE

1. Charbon
2. Cuisine
3. Office
4. Escalier de service
5. W.C.
6. Chambres
7. Dégagements
8. Grand Escalier
9. Antichambres
10. Salle à manger
11. Courettes
12. Cabinet de travail
13. Salon
14. Salle de bains

PREMIER ETAGE ET BALCON

PREMIER ETAGE (AVANT-CORPS)

REZ-DE-CHAUSSEE

Échelle de

Gelis-Didot et Lambert d.   CH. GIRAULT, ARCH.ᵗᵉ   Héliogravure Dujardin

MAISON

12ᵇⁱˢ PLACE DE LABORDE

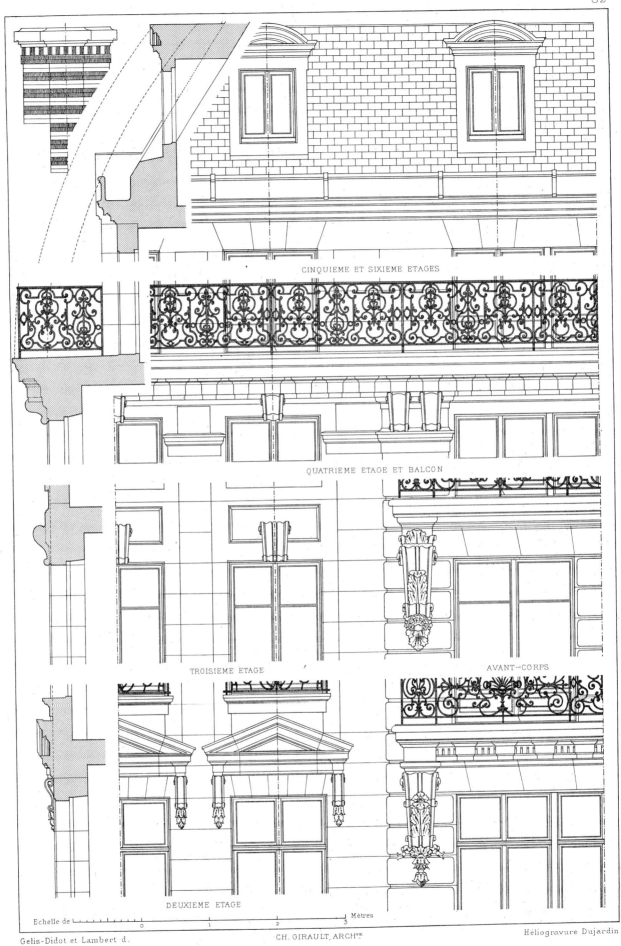

CINQUIEME ET SIXIEME ETAGES

QUATRIEME ETAGE ET BALCON

TROISIEME ETAGE

AVANT-CORPS

DEUXIEME ETAGE

Echelle de 0 1 2 3 Mètres

Gelis-Didot et Lambert d.

CH. GIRAULT, ARCH.ᵗᵉ

Héliogravure Dujardin

MAISON

12 ᵇⁱˢ PLACE DE LABORDE

63

Gélis-Didot et Lambert d.   GUADET, ARCH.   Héliog.ᵉ Dujardin

MAISON
240ᵇⁱˢ BOULEVARD Sᵗ GERMAIN

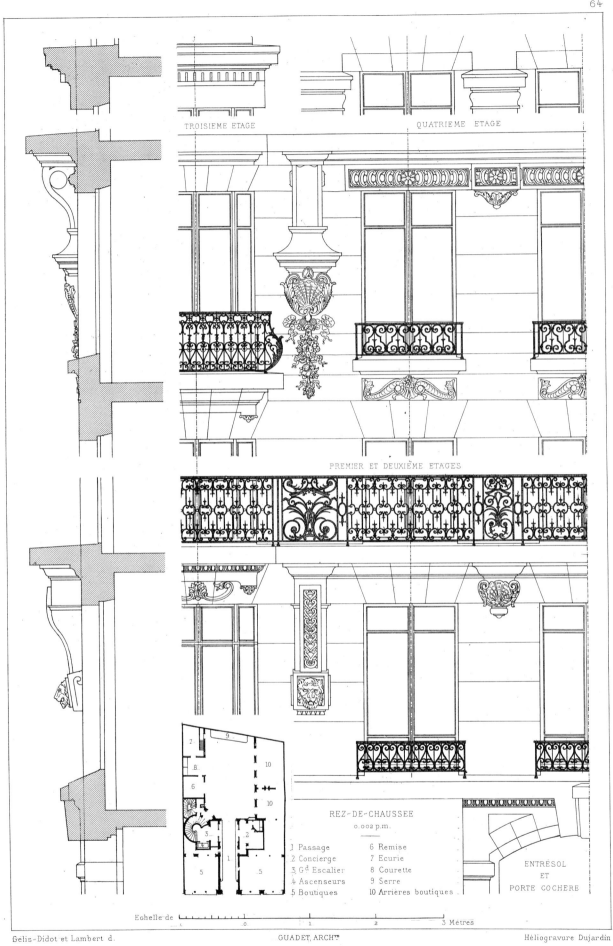

TROISIEME ETAGE

QUATRIEME ETAGE

PREMIER ET DEUXIÈME ETAGES

REZ–DE–CHAUSSEE

0.002 p.m.

1 Passage 6 Remise
2 Concierge 7 Ecurie
3 G.d Escalier 8 Courette
4 Ascenseurs 9 Serre
5 Boutiques 10 Arrières boutiques

ENTRÉSOL
ET
PORTE COCHERE

Echelle de ⊢⊢⊢⊢⊢⊢⊢⊢⊢⊢⊢⊢⊢⊢⊢⊢⊢⊢⊢⊢⊢⊢⊢ 3 Métres

Gelis-Didot et Lambert d.   GUADET, ARCH.te   Héliogravure Dujardin

MAISON
240.bis BOULEVARD SAINT-GERMAIN

Gélis-Didot et Lambert d.

GOUNY, ARCHᵀᴱ

Héliogᵗᵉ Dujardin

Cⁱᴱ DES CHEMINS DE FER DE L'EST

BATIMENTS D'ADMINISTRATION

FAUBOURG ST DENIS, 144 146.

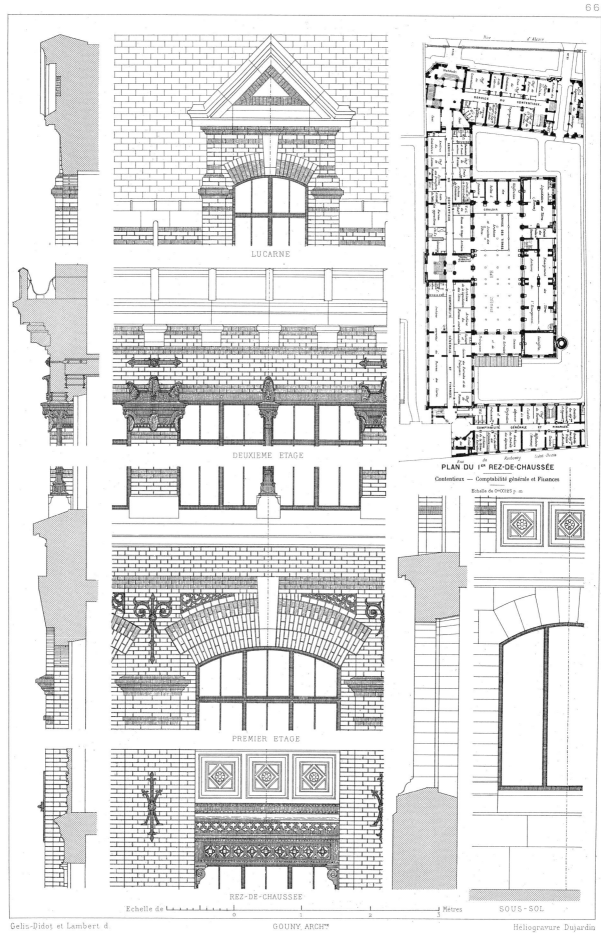

LUCARNE

DEUXIEME ETAGE

PREMIER ETAGE

REZ-DE-CHAUSSEE

PLAN DU 1ᴱᴿ REZ-DE-CHAUSSÉE

Contentieux — Comptabilité générale et Finances

Echelle de 0ᵐ0012·5 p·m

SOUS-SOL

Echelle de 0 1 2 3 Mètres

Gelis-Didot et Lambert d.   GOUNY, ARCHᵀᴱ   Héliogravure Dujardin

Cⁱᴱ DES CHEMINS DE FER DE L'EST

BATIMENTS D'ADMINISTRATION

FAUBOURG Sᵀ DENIS, 144, 146.

Gelis-Didot et Lambert d.   GOUNY, ARCH^TE   Héliogravure Dujardin.

C^IE DES CHEMINS DE FER DE L'EST

BATIMENTS D'ADMINISTRATION

RUE D'ALSACE, 21, 23.

QUATRIEME ETAGE

LUCARNE

TROISIEME ETAGE

DEUXIEME ETAGE_PAVILLON

DEUXIEME ETAGE

REZ-DE-CHAUSSEE

Echelle de 0 1 2 3 Mètres

Gelis-Didot et Lambert d.

GOUNY, ARCH.ᵗᵉ

Héliogravure Dujardin

Cᴵᴱ DES CHEMINS DE FER DE L'EST

BATIMENTS D'ADMINISTRATION

RUE D'ALSACE, 21, 23.

Gelis Didot et Lambert d.   LALOUX, ARCH.ᵀᴱ   Héliogravure Dujardin

MAISON

64, RUE DES PETITS-CHAMPS

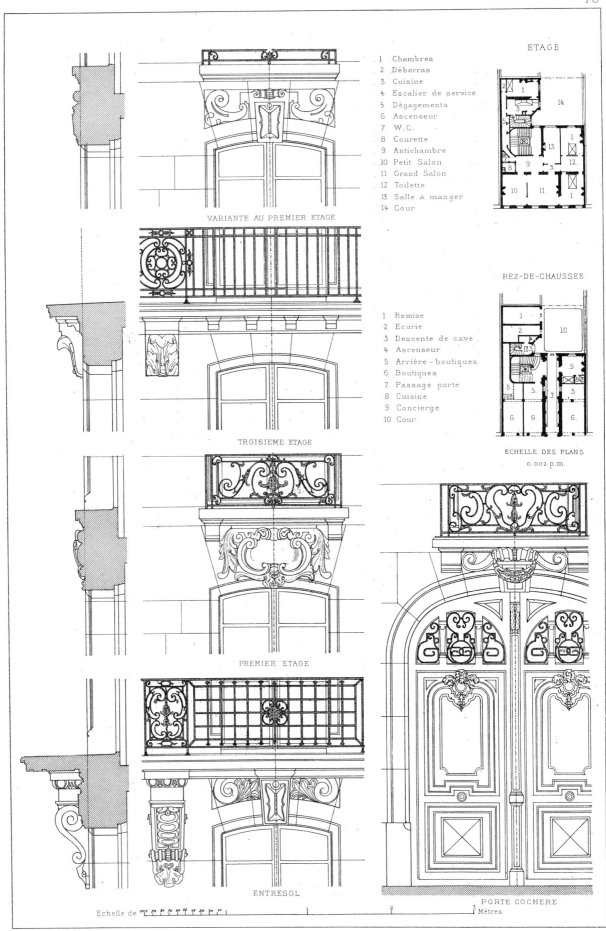

ETAGE

1 Chambres
2 Débarras
3 Cuisine
4 Escalier de service
5 Dégagements
6 Ascenseur
7 W.C.
8 Courette
9 Antichambre
10 Petit Salon
11 Grand Salon
12 Toilette
13 Salle à manger
14 Cour

VARIANTE AU PREMIER ETAGE

REZ-DE-CHAUSSEE

1 Remise
2 Ecurie
3 Descente de cave
4 Ascenseur
5 Arrière-boutiques
6 Boutiques
7 Passage porte
8 Cuisine
9 Concierge
10 Cour

TROISIEME ETAGE

ECHELLE DES PLANS
0.002 p.m.

PREMIER ETAGE

ENTRESOL

PORTE COCHERE

Echelle de ⏜ Mètres

Gelis-Didot et Lambert d.   LALOUX, ARCHᵀᴱ   Héliogravure Dujardin.

MAISON

64, RUE DES PETITS-CHAMPS

Gelis-Didot et Lambert d. ESCALIER, ARCH.ᵗᵉ Héliogravure Dujardin

MAISON

10, RUE DE TURIN

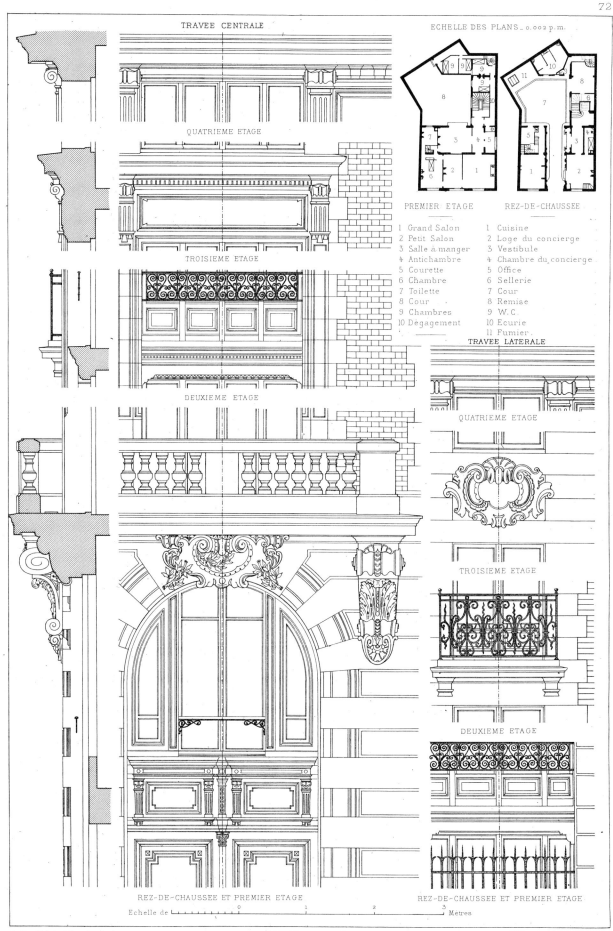

TRAVEE CENTRALE

ECHELLE DES PLANS_0.002 p.m.

QUATRIEME ETAGE

TROISIEME ETAGE

DEUXIEME ETAGE

PREMIER ETAGE

1 Grand Salon
2 Petit Salon
3 Salle à manger
4 Antichambre
5 Courette
6 Chambre
7 Toilette
8 Cour
9 Chambres
10 Dégagement

REZ-DE-CHAUSSEE

1 Cuisine
2 Loge du concierge
3 Vestibule
4 Chambre du concierge
5 Office
6 Sellerie
7 Cour
8 Remise
9 W.C.
10 Ecurie
11 Fumier

TRAVEE LATERALE

QUATRIEME ETAGE

TROISIEME ETAGE

DEUXIEME ETAGE

REZ-DE-CHAUSSEE ET PREMIER ETAGE

REZ-DE-CHAUSSEE ET PREMIER ETAGE

Echelle de ⊢⊢⊢⊢⊢⊢⊢ 0   1   2   3 Metres

Gelis-Didot et Lambert d.   ESCALIER, ARCH.ᵀᴱ   Héliogravure Dujardin

MAISON
10, RUE DE TURIN.

Gelis-Didot et Lambert d.   P. SEDILLE, ARCH.   Heliogravure Dujardin

MAISON

13, RUE VERNET

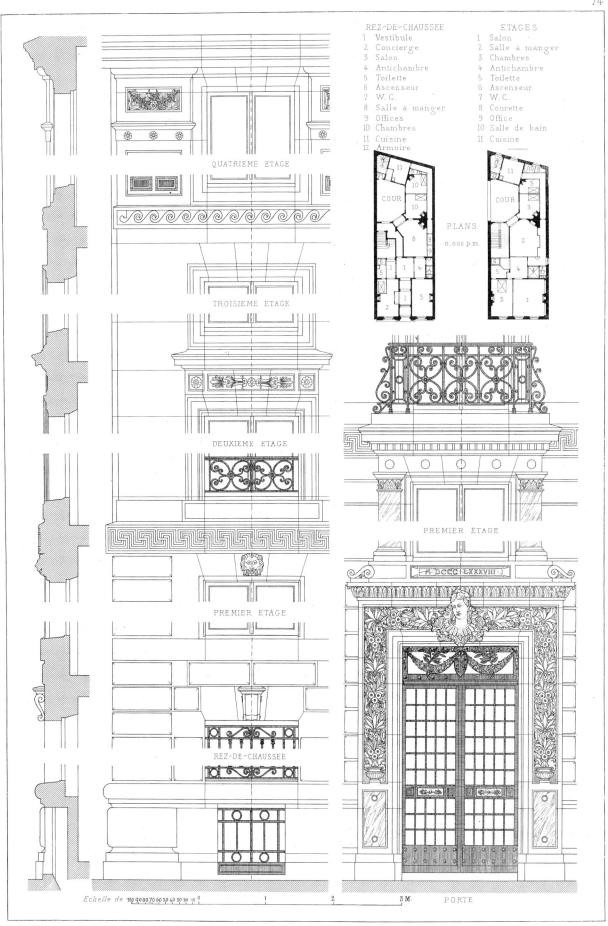

QUATRIEME ETAGE

TROISIEME ETAGE

DEUXIEME ETAGE

PREMIER ETAGE

REZ-DE-CHAUSSEE

REZ-DE-CHAUSSEE	ETAGES
1 Vestibule	1 Salon
2 Concierge	2 Salle à manger
3 Salon	3 Chambres
4 Antichambre	4 Antichambre
5 Toilette	5 Toilette
6 Ascenseur	6 Ascenseur
7 W. C.	7 W. C.
8 Salle à manger	8 Courette
9 Offices	9 Office
10 Chambres	10 Salle de bain
11 Cuisine	11 Cuisine
12 Armoire	

PLANS

0.002 p.m.

COUR

M·DCCC·LXXXVIII

PREMIER ETAGE

PORTE

Echelle de 100 90 80 70 60 50 40 30 20 10 0   1   2   3 M.

Gélis-Didot et Lambert d.   P. SEDILLE, ARCH.ᵀᴱ   Héliogravure Dujardin

MAISON

13, RUE VERNET

Gelis-Didot et Lambert d.   PASCAL, ARCH^{te}   Héliogravure Dujardin

MAISON

197, BOULEVARD SAINT-GERMAIN

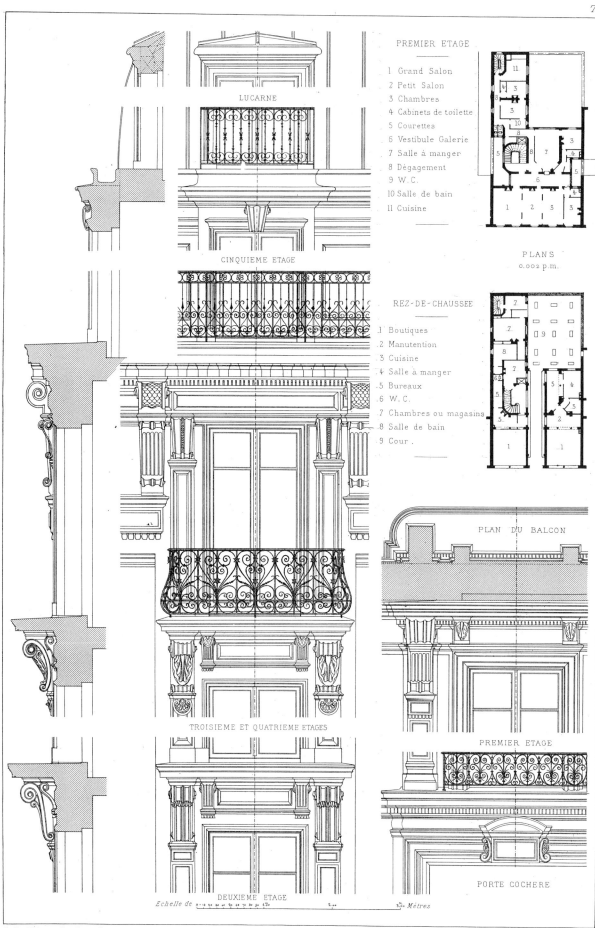

LUCARNE

CINQUIEME ETAGE

PREMIER ETAGE

1 Grand Salon
2 Petit Salon
3 Chambres
4 Cabinets de toilette
5 Courettes
6 Vestibule Galerie
7 Salle à manger
8 Dègagement
9 W.C.
10 Salle de bain
11 Cuisine

PLANS
0.002 p.m.

REZ-DE-CHAUSSEE

1 Boutiques
2 Manutention
3 Cuisine
4 Salle à manger
5 Bureaux
6 W.C.
7 Chambres ou magasins
8 Salle de bain
9 Cour.

TROISIEME ET QUATRIEME ETAGES

PLAN DU BALCON

PREMIER ETAGE

DEUXIEME ETAGE

Echelle de 0 10 20 30 40 50 60 70 80 90 1.00   2.00   3.00 Métres

PORTE COCHERE

Gelis-Didot et Lambert d.   PASCAL, ARCHᵗᵉ   Héliogravure Dujardin

MAISON

197, BOULEVARD Sᵗ GERMAIN

Gelis-Didot et Lambert d.

PASCAL, ARCH.ᵗᵉ

Héliogravure Dujardin

MAISON

105, RUE NOTRE-DAME-DES-CHAMPS

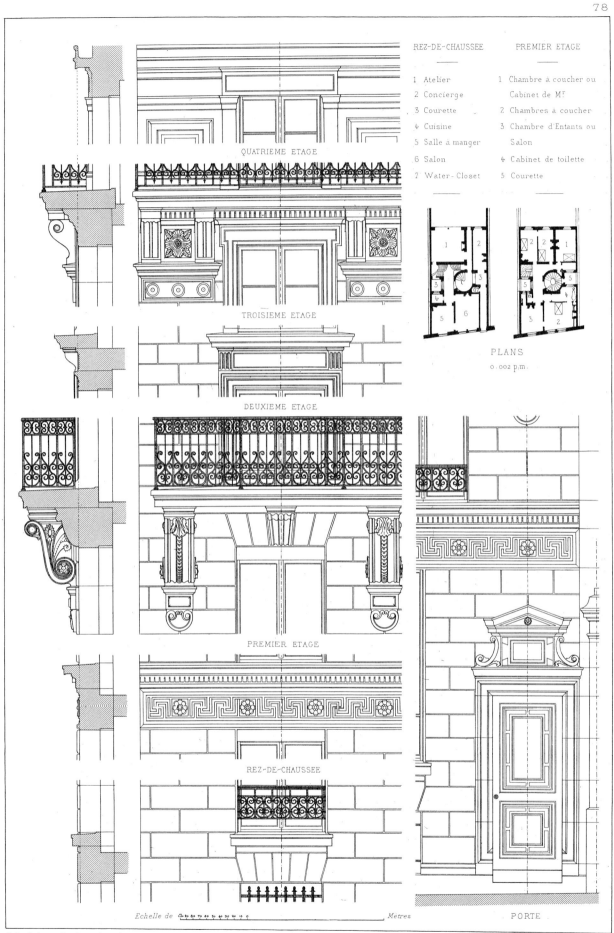

QUATRIEME ETAGE

TROISIEME ETAGE

DEUXIEME ETAGE

PREMIER ETAGE

REZ-DE-CHAUSSEE

REZ-DE-CHAUSSEE	PREMIER ETAGE
1 Atelier	1 Chambre à coucher ou
2 Concierge	Cabinet de Mr
3 Courette	2 Chambres à coucher
4 Cuisine	3 Chambre d'Enfants ou
5 Salle à manger	Salon
6 Salon	4 Cabinet de toilette
7 Water-Closet	5 Courette

PLANS

0.002 p.m.

PORTE

Echelle de   Metres

Gelis-Didot et Lambert d.   PASCAL, ARCHᵗᵉ   Héliogravure Dujardin

MAISON

105, RUE NOTRE-DAME DES CHAMPS

Gélis-Didot et Lambert d. CAHN-BOUSSON, ARCH.^{te} Héliogravure Dujardin

MAISON

32, RUE DU LUXEMBOURG

REZ-DE-CHAUSSÉE   PREMIER ETAGE

1 Vestibule d'entrée   1 Antichambre
2 Salle de billard   2 Grand Salon
3 Salle à manger   3 Petit Salon
4 Chambres à coucher   4 Salle à manger
5 Antichambre   5 Chambres à coucher
6 Office   6 Salle de bain
7 Grand Salon   7 Courette
8 Petit Salon
9 Concierge

QUATRIEME ETAGE

TROISIEME ETAGE

CINQUIEME ETAGE

DEUXIEME ETAGE

PREMIER ETAGE

PREMIER ETAGE

PORTE

Echelle de 100 50 0 1 2 3 Mètres

Gelis-Didot et Lambert d.   CAHN-BOUSSON, ARCH.TE   Héliogravure Dujardin

MAISON

32, RUE DU LUXEMBOURG

Gelis-Didot et Lambert d.   A. HERMANT, ARCH.ᵀᵉ   Héliogravure Dujardin

MAISON

63, BOULEVARD HAUSSMANN

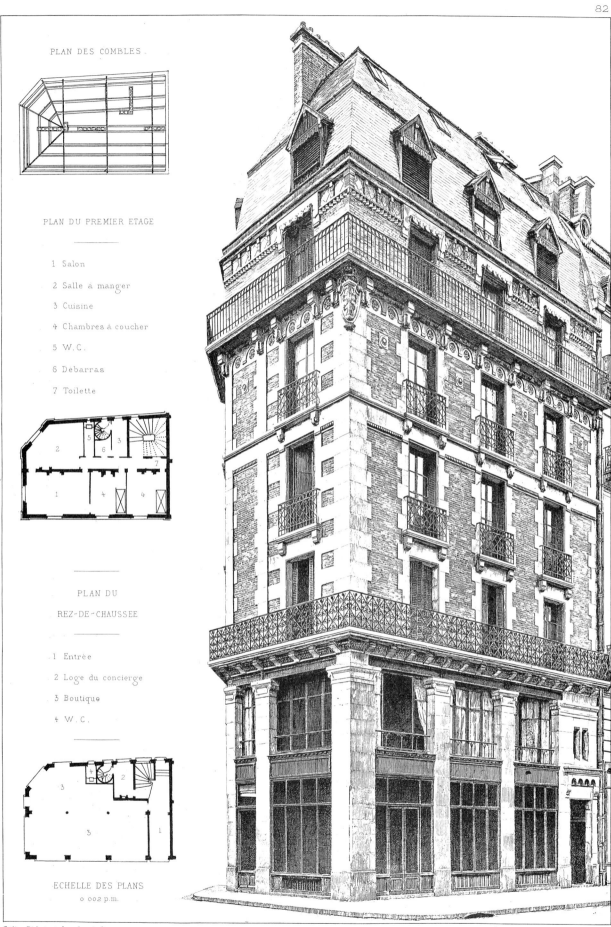

PLAN DES COMBLES.

PLAN DU PREMIER ETAGE

1 Salon

2 Salle à manger

3 Cuisine

4 Chambres à coucher

5 W.C.

6 Debarras

7 Toilette

PLAN DU

REZ-DE-CHAUSSEE

1 Entrée

2 Loge du concierge

3 Boutique

4 W.C.

ECHELLE DES PLANS

0 002 p.m.

Gélis-Didot et Lambert d.   L. MAGNE, ARCH.^TE   Héliogravure Dujardin

MAISON

17, RUE DES PYRAMIDES

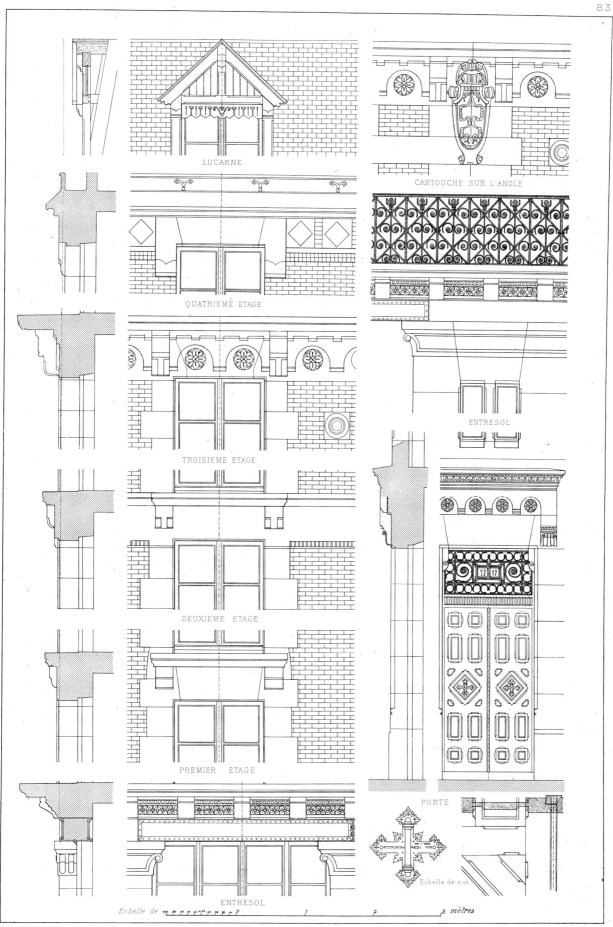

LUCARNE

CARTOUCHE SUR L'ANGLE

QUATRIÈME ETAGE

TROISIEME ETAGE

ENTRESOL

DEUXIEME ETAGE

PREMIER ETAGE

PORTE

ENTRESOL

Echelle de 0.10

Echelle de   1   2   3 mètres

Gelis-Didot et Lambert d.   L. MAGNE, ARCH^{TE}   Héliogravure Dujardin

MAISON

17, RUE DES PYRAMIDES.

Gelis-Didot et Lambert d. RAULIN, ARCHᵗᵉ Héliogᵗᵉ Dujardin

MAISON DE COMMERCE

13, RUE D'UZES

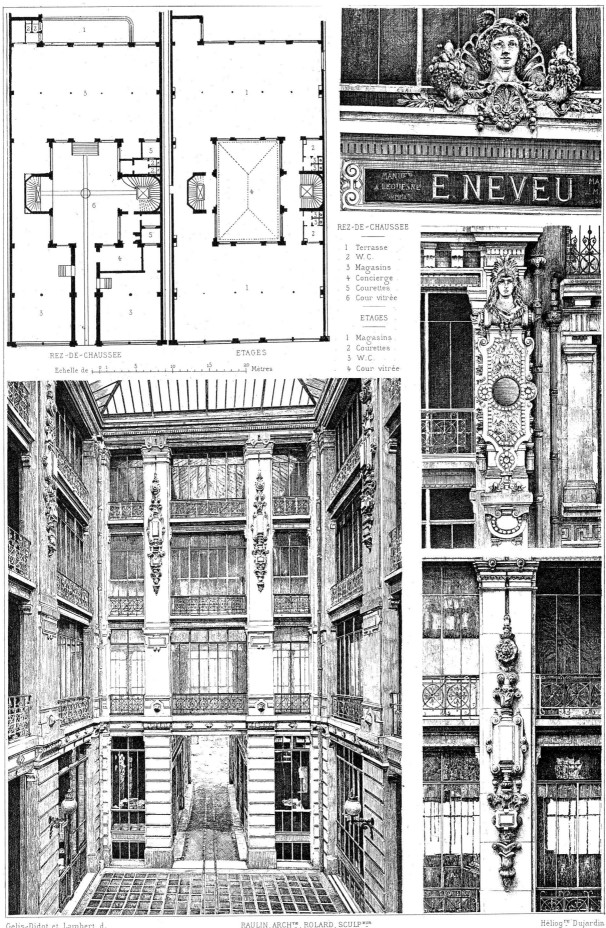

REZ-DE-CHAUSSEE

1 Terrasse
2 W. C.
3 Magasins
4 Concierge
5 Courettes
6 Cour vitrée

ETAGES

1 Magasins
2 Courettes
3 W.C.
4 Cour vitrée

REZ-DE-CHAUSSEE   ETAGES

Echelle de   0 1   5   10   15   20   Mètres

Gelis-Didot et Lambert d.   RAULIN, ARCH.ᵀᴱ, ROLARD, SCULP.ᴱᵁᴿ   Héliog.ʳᵉ Dujardin

MAISON DE COMMERCE

13, RUE D'UZES

Gelis-Didot et Lambert d.   L. MAGNE, ARCH.te   Héliogravure Dujardin

MAISON
RUE DU LOUVRE ET RUE ETIENNE MARÇEL

LUCARNE

QUATRIEME ETAGE

PORTE, RUE D'ARGOUT

TROISIEME ETAGE ET FRISE

TROISIEME ETAGE ET FRISE

DEUXIEME ETAGE

PREMIER ETAGE

PLAN DE LA
CHARPENTE EN FER
0.002 p.m.

PREMIER ETAGE

0.002 p.m.

1 Vestibule
2 Salon
3 Salle à manger
4 Cuisine
5 Chambres à coucher
6 Cabinets
7 W. C.

REZ-DE-CHAUSSEE

0.002 p.m.

1 Escalier conduisant
aux étages
2 Escalier conduisant à
l'entresol
3 Concierge
4 Boutiques
5 Dependances

ENTRESOL

Echelle de   3 mètres

COLONNES EN
FONTE

Gelis-Didot et Lambert d.   L. MAGNE, ARCH.ᵗᵉ   Héliogravure Dujardin

MAISON

RUE DU LOUVRE ET RUE ETIENNE-MARCEL

Gelis-Didot et Lambert d. PAUL SEDILLE, ARCH.^{TE} Héliogravure Dujardin

MAISON

28, BOULEVARD MALESHERBES

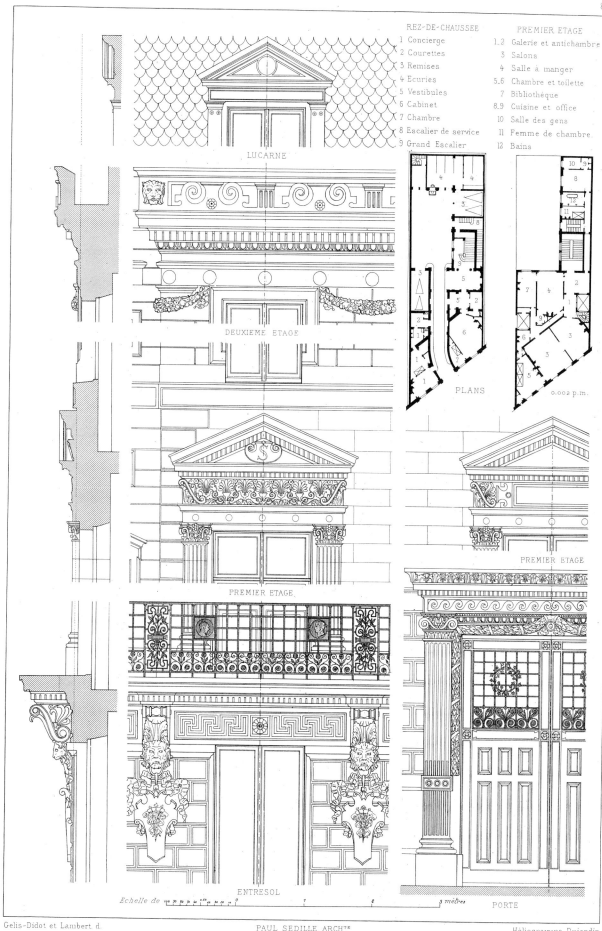

REZ-DE-CHAUSSEE
1 Concierge
2 Courettes
3 Remises
4 Ecuries
5 Vestibules
6 Cabinet
7 Chambre
8 Escalier de service
9 Grand Escalier

PREMIER ETAGE
1.2 Galerie et antichambre
3 Salons
4 Salle à manger
5.6 Chambre et toilette
7 Bibliothèque
8.9 Cuisine et office
10 Salle des gens
11 Femme de chambre
12 Bains

LUCARNE

DEUXIEME ETAGE

PLANS

0.002 p.m.

PREMIER ETAGE

PREMIER ETAGE

ENTRESOL

Echelle de

3 mètres

PORTE

Gelis-Didot et Lambert d.

PAUL SEDILLE, ARCH.TE

Héliogravure Dujardin

MAISON
28, BOULEVARD MALESHERBES

HERMANT PERE ET FILS, ARCH^{TES}

MAISON

116, BOULEVARD SAINT-GERMAIN ET RUE DANTON

FAÇADE SUR LE BOULEVARD.

MAISON
116, BOULEVARD SAINT-GERMAIN ET RUE DANTON

FAÇADE SUR LA RUE DANTON.

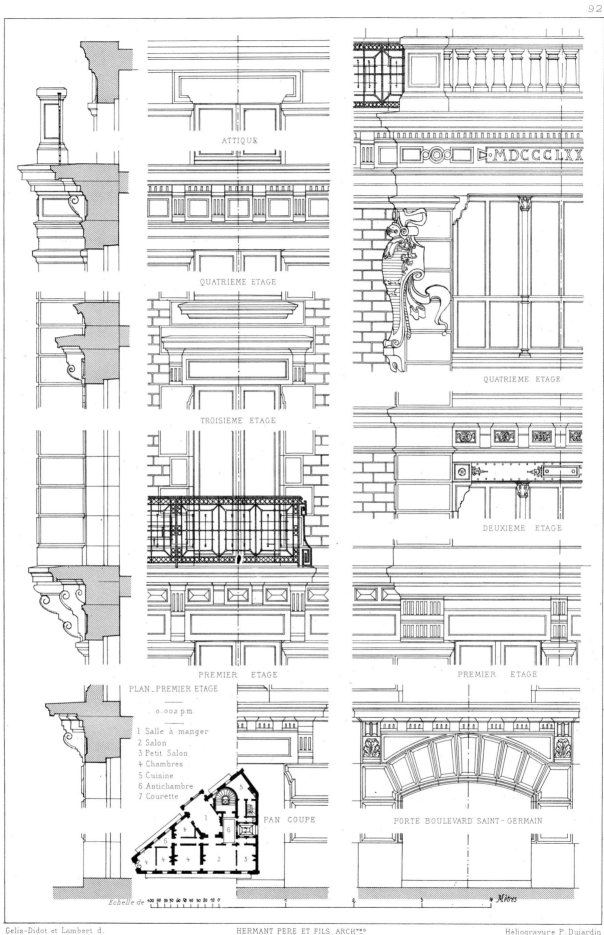

ATTIQUE

QUATRIEME ETAGE

TROISIEME ETAGE

PREMIER ETAGE

MDCCCLXX

QUATRIEME ETAGE

DEUXIEME ETAGE

PREMIER ETAGE

PLAN _ PREMIER ETAGE

0.002 p.m.

1 Salle à manger
2 Salon
3 Petit Salon
4 Chambres
5 Cuisine
6 Antichambre
7 Courette

PAN COUPE

PORTE BOULEVARD SAINT - GERMAIN

Echelle de 100 90 80 70 60 50 40 30 20 10 0   Mètres

Gelis-Didot et Lambert d.

HERMANT PERE ET FILS, ARCH.^{tes}

Héliogravure P. Dujardin

MAISON

116, BOULEVARD SAINT-GERMAIN ET RUE DANTON

Gelis-Didot et Lambert d.   DUVAL, ARCH^TE   Héliogravure Dujardin.

MAISON

61, RUE BONAPARTE ET 12 PLACE SAINT-SULPICE.

FAÇADE PLACE SAINT-SULPICE.

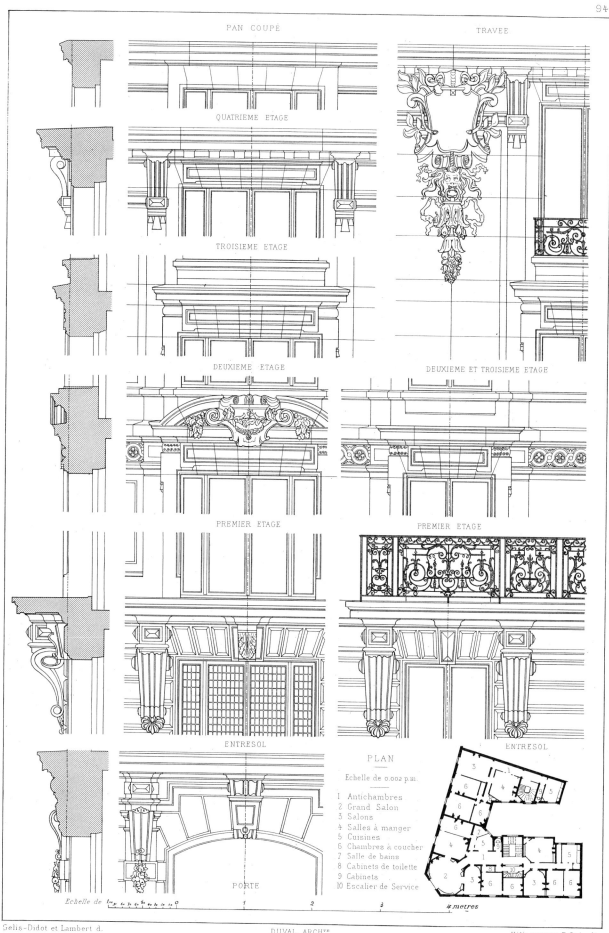

PAN COUPÉ

TRAVÉE

QUATRIEME ETAGE

TROISIEME ETAGE

DEUXIEME ETAGE

DEUXIEME ET TROISIEME ETAGE

PREMIER ETAGE

PREMIER ETAGE

ENTRESOL

ENTRESOL

PLAN

Echelle de 0.002 p.m.

1 Antichambres
2 Grand Salon
3 Salons
4 Salles à manger
5 Cuisines
6 Chambres à coucher
7 Salle de bains
8 Cabinets de toilette
9 Cabinets
10 Escalier de Service

PORTE

Echelle de 1ᵐ 90 80 70 60 50 40 30 20 10 0   1   2   3   4 metres

Gelis-Didot et Lambert d.

DUVAL, ARCHᵗᵉ

Héliogravure P. Dujardin

MAISON

61, RUE BONAPARTE ET 12, PLACE SAINT-SULPICE

Gelis-Didot et Lambert d.   BREASSON, ARCH^{TE}   Héliogravure P. Dujardin.

MAISON

125, BOULEVARD MONTPARNASSE

CINQUIEME ETAGE

TROISIEME ETAGE

1888 89

PREMIER ETAGE

PLAN PREMIER ETAGE
-0.002 p.m.-

LEGENDE

1 Salle à manger
2 Salon
3 Chambres
4 Cabinet de travail
5 Salle de bains
6 Bureau
7 Antichambre
8 Escalier particulier
9 Escalier des locataires
10 Courette
11 Cuisine
12 Débarras

REZ-DE-CHAUSSEE

Echelle de 0   7   8 mètres

Gelis-Didot et Lambert d.   BREASSON, ARCH.ᵗᵉ   Héliogravure Dujardin

MAISON
125, BOULEVARD MONTPARNASSE

Gelis-Didot et Lambert d.   P. HENEUX, ARCH^{TE}   Héliogravure P. Dujardin

MAISON

96, BOULEVARD DES BATIGNOLLES

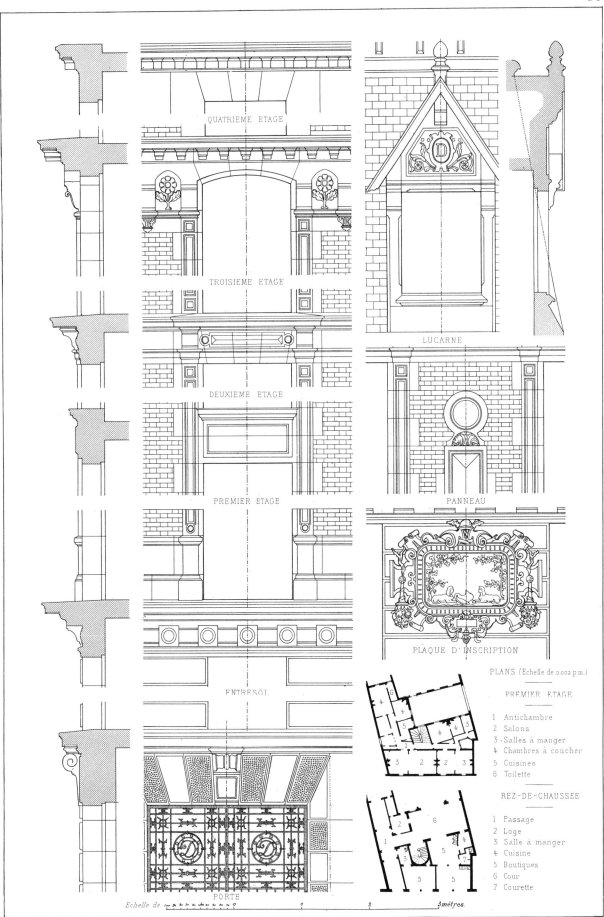

QUATRIEME ETAGE

TROISIEME ETAGE

DEUXIEME ETAGE

PREMIER ETAGE

ENTRESOL

PORTE

LUCARNE

PANNEAU

PLAQUE D'INSCRIPTION

PLANS (Echelle de 0.002 p.m.)

PREMIER ETAGE

1 Antichambre
2 Salons
3 Salles à manger
4 Chambres à coucher
5 Cuisines
6 Toilette

REZ-DE-CHAUSSEE

1 Passage
2 Loge
3 Salle à manger
4 Cuisine
5 Boutiques
6 Cour
7 Courette

Echelle de .... 0 .... 1 .... 2 .... 3 mètres.

Gelis-Didot et Lambert d.   P. HENEUX, ARCH.ᵗᵉ   Héliog.ʳᵉ P. Dujardin.

MAISON
96, BOULEVARD DES BATIGNOLLES.

Gelis-Didot et Lambert d.   A. CHAPELAIN, ARCH.TE   Heliog.re. P. Dujardin

MAISON
11, RUE DE SOLFERINO

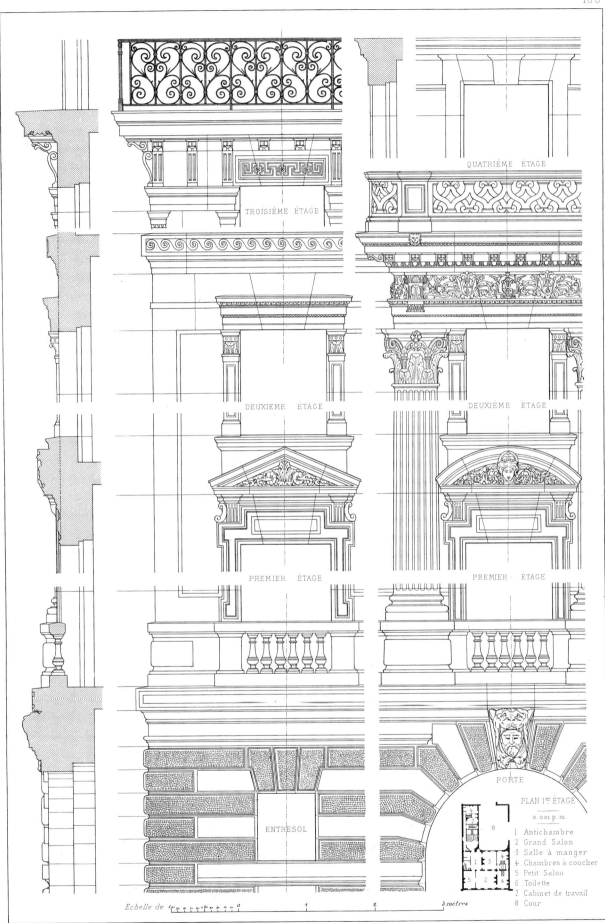

QUATRIÈME ÉTAGE

TROISIÈME ÉTAGE

DEUXIÈME ÉTAGE

DEUXIÈME ÉTAGE

PREMIER ÉTAGE

PREMIER ÉTAGE

ENTRESOL

PORTE

PLAN 1ᵉʳ ÉTAGE

0.001 p.m.

1 Antichambre
2 Grand Salon
3 Salle à manger
4 Chambres à coucher
5 Petit Salon
6 Toilette
7 Cabinet de travail
8 Cour

Echelle de 1ᵐ   0   1   2   3 mètres

Gelis-Didot et Lambert d.   A. CHAPELAIN, ARCHᵀᴱ   Héliogʳᵉ P. Dujardin

MAISON
11, RUE DE SOLFERINO.